Gerald —

I am grateful
you're here and
living the life you
were meant to live —

Blessings,
Jane

Acclaim for *Kids in Jail*

"Jane Guttman gives voice to one of the 21st century's most marginalized populations—incarcerated children—and she does so with compassion and great insight. The result is a powerful narrative that provides a rare glimpse of what life is like on the *inside* for more than 70,000 kids across the United States. It is beautifully done."

Tamar R. Birckhead, Associate Professor and Director of Clinical Programs at the University of North Carolina School of Law

• • •

"Thank you for shining a light on one of the greatest travesties of our time-the violation of youth rights. Wherever kids are in jail, they will recognize the deep and moving feelings expressed here. For the rest of us, we will be moved to action."

Mary Beth Tinker, RN
Plaintiff in landmark students' rights case, *Tinker v. Des Moines Independent School Board* (1969)

• • •

"You are lighting hope in millions of hearts."

Julieanne Collins, LCSW, Former Juvenile Hall Therapist

• • •

"Jane's wonderful work, *Kids in Jail*, offers the true narrative of children who come into contact with the law. Having been failed by so many individuals, systems, and policies, many children who enter our justice system are simply demonized and discarded forever. Kids are not miniature adults, and they should not be held to the same level of culpability and accountability as adults. And most importantly, we should never lose sight of children's capacity for positive change. *Kids in Jail*, so eloquently and poetically, conveys this truth."

Xavier McElrath-Bey, Youth Justice Advocate / ICAN Coordinator
Campaign for the Fair Sentencing of Youth

• • •

"Jane Guttman's groundbreaking work, *Kids in Jail,* eloquently addresses the quest to ensure the human dignity and civil rights of incarcerated youth. Jane's passion to protect and inspire youth is on every page."

Elisa Gusdal, Artist, Educator and Union Organizer

• • •

"Jane Guttman gives the world a glance at the amazing talents hidden away at juvenile correctional facilities throughout this country. She is also a voice for all of the dedicated teachers and correctional officers within those programs."

Mike Lepore M.A., Former Correctional Officer, Fresno County Probation; Teacher, Fresno County Office of Education

• • •

"In her powerful book, *Kids in Jail,* Jane Guttman captures both spectral edges of this population, bringing to life the fragility and woundedness that carry these young people to places of deep despair as well as the resilience and determination that will lead many of them out. Beautifully written and with a pitch-perfect ear for the voices of her subjects, *Kids in Jail* serves as a brilliant tribute to the lives of our nation's most underserved children."

Bethany Casarjian, Ph.D., Clinical Director of Youth Services
The Lionheart Foundation

• • •

"*Kids in Jail* is a must read. Told in the voices of the children behind bars it is fresh, insightful and revealing. My heart was touched by the stories of these children."

Kenneth L. Decroo, Ph.D., Principal
Mary Putnam Henck Intermediate School, Lake Arrowhead, CA

• • •

"*Kids in Jail* is a book that needs to be read by anyone who cares about kids. Jane's poignant prose combined with the poetry for these wounded children will stir the most cynical heart. There but for the grace of God go all of us."

Cindy Sanford, Author
Letters to a Lifer: The Boy 'Never to Be Released' (2015)

· · ·

"*Kids in Jail*, a haunting, agonizing picture of life for America's children in the jail system, will affect you deeply. I want to know more. Hopefully the children's cries will echo into your heart until you are moved to show up. May God Bless this book as it travels the world."

Diana Nice-Michel
Former Student, Apollo High School (1974)

· · ·

"What a beautiful tribute to your street soldiers, including the young women. Your prose is as lyrical and haunting as your poetry. Your language lets the reader viscerally experience the soul of your students. As I read your poetic narrations, I wanted to share them aloud with whomever was around. Enlightening."

Lesley Farmer, Chair of Advanced Studies in Education and Counseling and Coordinator of Librarianship Program
California State University, Long Beach

· · ·

"Jane Guttman presents a picture of confinement that begs for reform. The fictionalized, yet realistic depictions of detainees inform the reader of what lives can become in only a few short years. The detainees even hint at possible solutions. Now we must pay attention."

Dee Gerken, MSN, Nurse Practitioner-Certified

· · ·

"I read Jane Guttman's *Kids in Jail* with great interest and understanding. Her words should be mandatory reading for anyone dealing with marginalized kids in our society. We must recognize the need to inspire kids, even those trapped in the "system" to educate themselves. *Kids in Jail* is a must read."

Steve Nawojczyk, Juvenile Justice Advocate and Youth Violence Specialist

· · ·

"As a journalist, for the past 25 years I have travelled to some of the world's poorest and most violent countries to cover child rights' issues. Some of the most heartbreaking and infuriating stories I've heard have been told to me by incarcerated children in the United States. The systematic and state sanctioned forms of child abuse that go on in juvenile halls, such as long-term solitary confinement, are chilling. Jane Guttman has done something remarkable. Her verses bring home the sad truth about why most of these children are locked up in the first place, how it could have been avoided, and why it is so wrong to give up on them."

Carmilla Floyd, Director of Communications
World's Children's Prize Foundation

• • •

"Long before Barak Obama visited a Federal Penitentiary to shed light on the dark history of incarcerated life, Jane Guttman was writing the untold story from its most fragile voices – kids in those jails, silenced and forgotten. Jane Guttman gifts us by holding up the light as we progress to beautiful things ahead for the children of our beloved nation."

Megan Smith, California Alternative Educator

• • •

"What crushing burdens on the young! Thank you for jumping into the ditch to help them bear it. It is profoundly important work."

Barbara Frances
Community Advocate

• • •

"*Kids in Jail* champions youth in custody and influences those who care about them. Jane Guttman's readership will be inspired to join those devoted to reforming our flawed juvenile justice system. This rare view of life *inside* awakens hearts and minds to the plight of our deeply disenfranchised and underserved children."

Azim Khamisa, Author, Speaker, and Founder of the Tariq Khamisa Foundation

• • •

Kids *in* Jail

A PORTRAIT OF LIFE WITHOUT MERCY

JANE GUTTMAN

JMJ Publishing
Lake Arrowhead, California

Printed on acid-free paper.

First Printing, 2016

JMJ Publishing
ISBN: 978-0-9672861-1-2

Front cover photograph by Bob Riha Jr.
Back cover photograph by Richard Ross

ALSO BY JANE GUTTMAN

The Gift Wrapped in Sorrow: A Mother's Quest for Healing

My infinite respect and appreciation to the extraordinary correctional officers that I have met and collaborated with over the past 15 years, bringing heart and humanity to their positions, while keeping kids safe and inspired. I honor these civil servants as they stand ready to protect and redirect so many lost youth. Although they must remain unnamed, they are fully honored and hailed in the spirit of justice and partnership. To "the others" — those that have forsaken humanity, justice and integrity — you are fuel for system reform and mercy.

In Tribute

Patty Wallace—one of my first troubled students—now, almost fifty years later, her fierce and loving spirit lives strongly in my memory. May the tragedy and triumph of her life and her death stay alive in my teaching and service.

My students in custody—I remain humbled by your spirits, haunted by your cries.

A. and R.—I carry you in my heart as you live life behind bars.

Alfonso and so many others—I applaud your strides in rising out of the dark beginnings of your life.

Kenneth Crawford—you inspire and awe with the great accomplishments you make in your *life without parole life*. Your heart and spirit soar.

Kalief Browder—may your life and death lead us to benevolence and justice for those behind bars.

The late Debra Botello—my inspiring colleague and mentor. Thank you for guiding me.

The incarcerated beings on this earth—your struggles and your anguish rush to the core of my heart, compelling me to stand beside every justice advocate as we bring the inhumanity to rest.

Contents

Foreword

In her beautifully poignant book, *Kids in Jail*, Jane Guttman brings us deeply into the inner lives of some of our nation's most disconnected and disenfranchised youth. Each verse she has crafted burns brightly and illuminates countless often unheard human experiences. In the end, what she creates is an entire constellation of lives that exist, but are rarely seen by those of us not living within their universe. Only the very few, those working on the *inside*, are privy to the complex voices of these young people. And even fewer would be capable of rendering, with such skill and humanity a literary history of those who otherwise might slip into adulthood as just a statistic of school dropout, teenage pregnancy, or incarceration. *Kids in Jail* captures the unrelenting resilience, undeniable dignity, and deeply fragile lives of youth who are growing up within a system that is by and large incapable of meeting their profound emotional and social needs, a system that warehouses rather than heals.

My path first crossed with Jane's when she brought Lionheart's book for at-risk youth, *Power Source: Taking Charge of Your Life*, into her library at a California court school. *Power Source* is written for the very youth Jane lends voice to in *Kids in Jail* – youth born into vicious cycles of poverty, abuse, neglect, drug dependency, and the criminal justice system. As a teacher librarian, Jane was elated to discover *Power Source,* which provided her students with the essential tools for transformation, and became the most requested book with her readership. Jane's passion for mitigating her students' suffering led her to Lionheart's resources.

For nearly 25 years, the Lionheart Foundation, which I founded and direct, has also harnessed the power of language to bring hope, insight, and peace to the men, women and youth caught in the interlaced web of poverty and the criminal justice system. At the core of Lionheart's programming are three books written for and to prisoners, youth in the criminal justice system, and high-risk teen parents that meld first-person stories with evidence-based, social-emotional learning. For many prisoners and youth in secure detention centers, these books have been a conduit to personal growth and transformation, as I believe *Kids in Jail* will be for youth in custody.

In the last decade, the importance of emotional literacy has gained increased recognition in the scientific community, as well as in the general public. Studies abound pointing to emotional literacy's impact on social adjustment, success at work, and a wide array of measures of psychological well-being. But unlike math or reading, emotional literacy remains outside of the domain of most schools, especially those in the poorest communities where educational systems struggle to meet the most modest standards. Unfortunately, this doubly disadvantages our most vulnerable youth, those coming from homes where parental absence, addiction, violence or mental illness limit caregivers' ability to model and teach healthy emotional regulation. Furthermore, researchers now know that trauma derails children and adolescents' ability to develop healthy emotional literacy skills by forcing them to respond to threatening environments with violence or escape. Youth often come to jail for demonstrating the very behaviors that have served to keep them alive. The role of emotional literacy is to help build skills that empower them not simply to survive, but to thrive.

While these youth must contend with almost unimaginable adversity, they simultaneously face the most typical of adolescent tasks such as discovering who they are, navigating intimate relationships, and thinking about their futures. It is both Jane's and Lionheart's belief that social-emotional learning offers a path toward a future of hope and integrity. By helping youth learn to manage their emotions, develop the capacity for empathy, and embrace personal responsibility, they develop the skills necessary to break these toxic intergenerational cycles. Further, as they gain a deeper understanding of self beyond the labels they have been assigned, they shed the shame that has informed their view of who they are. For the developing adolescent, moving out of the shadow of shame is critical. Without this shift, he or she will continue to act in destructive ways that are in alignment with this misinformed view of self.

For those of us who have worked directly with the youth Jane represents in these inspired and expertly crafted poems, our hearts will resonate with the stories we have held for other young people. We will recognize their yearning to connect and the approach-avoidance style of those who want to trust, but have rightly learned to be wary. Regardless of how we come to this book, reading it opens a door that cannot be closed. Whether we live in their universe or not, these are our children. We will bear the consequences if their pain ends in violence and destruction, just as will we benefit if they heal the wounds of their past.

Robin Casarjian
The Lionheart Foundation
Boston, Massachusetts

Preface

It goes like this. Teaching is touching life.
— Jaime Escalante

One decade has lapsed since *Kids in Jail* first evolved. *Lola, William, Angel* and *Sophie* emerged to signify hundreds of kids I had known in those early years. They were a testimony to the collective trauma that I witnessed daily and could not speak of. As the words filled the pages, I was captivated by the courage, resilience and exquisite spirits of countless youth. In absorbing their realities, I plunged to the depths of despair for the fractures inherent in each, and have been stirred to hasten the reform that must ensue on behalf of human decency and justice.

The silence roars. The universal, unspoken code that disallows discussion of the treatment of the youth conceals the harm. Educators, as guests of probation, are accountable for every rule and prescription, and must comply to prevent being escorted from the facility or being refused entry, although employed by a separate agency. Restriction of dialogue is one such directive. Regardless of this convention, and in support of over 70K kids in custody in our nation, the collection for kids in custody will roar.

For many years, unaware of any indiscretion, I read *William* to classes that I visited during my tenure as a teacher librarian. Two responses were common. The kids would ask, "Which kid wrote that?" Then, as I shared that I was the author of the piece, the question became, "How did you know? How did you know *our* journey?" On one occasion, the room was remarkably silent as I read, and I could hear the students holding every word, and then at the end, raising their hands, asking their teacher, "Can we applaud?" In those times, a kid would raise his hand and say, "*I'm* William, really, *I'm* William!"

In 2015, and prior to knowing I was not permitted to share with students, I read *Sophie* to a class of young women in custody. The moment, now carved into my being, was a symphony of hearts and spirits, a true oneness as reader and listeners merged into the essence of what *Sophie* signified, and who she became to them. I see their faces, soaring to each word as a gift of confirmation to their lives and to their struggles. Shortly after this, I was directed by the school not to discuss the book with either students or staff, and to follow the categorical probation directive not to talk about the treatment of the youth.

Heart and conscience prevail and herein are the composite verses in honor of over one million kids that have endured custody in our nation since the day I began my correctional education journey. Although the despair is still painfully present, the decree for transforming the system is the prevailing ethic.

One absolute lesson I have learned in 15 years of teaching *inside* a juvenile jail is that all the children of the world belong to us. As I walk inside, I must bring the tools of humanity: an open heart, compassion, wisdom, courage, a spirit to listen and then foster transformation for kids who stray far from the path of dignity and well-being. Most of the kids, brutally fractured by their lives from the cradle to the booking cell at juvenile hall, reel from the crushing traumas and stumble toward a bleak future. Reversing the course of a childhood spent in custody requires our bold advocacy, with spirits shrouded in hope, steadfast to mentor, inspire and demand justice. In their land of turmoil and despair, our campaigning brings many youth back to the mainstream of life, awakening their quest to claim life and living.

If we look deeply enough into the eyes and heart of a kid in custody, we are compelled to go further than our contract asks. We must seek deeper solutions to the crisis of housing children in barbed wire and barren cells, often abundant with unforgiving guardianship. Many kids in custody struggle with severe mental health conditions, others with serious substance addiction. Where are the programs to treat these wounded and mentally ill children and adolescents? How can jail contribute to their healing or to building a life of purpose and well-being? We are faced with a compelling national crisis for our youth. From one border of our nation to another, kids are locked into circumstances that can defeat and destroy their futures.

I've had to toughen up to work in a juvenile hall facility. Being a frontline witness isn't easy. A colleague that I respect deeply had to leave for the inhumanity of it all. We've heard some scathing stories in those lost childhoods. Kids burned, abandoned, abused, molested, neglected, born addicted, parents in jail, parents addicted; and what about no home, no food, no guidance, and at times, no love. Add the ravages of mental illness and addiction. Then, the nightmare of a child seeing a parent commit suicide, or a mother murdered, beaten, or raped. After surviving these horrors, we inflict incarceration, rather than deliver interventions that could reverse the sting of such foreboding stories.

Once in custody, there are atrocities. Appalling conditions surface throughout the country. Consider kids on suicide watch beaten, sprayed, stripped, and then left in dark spaces, sometimes without heat, even in severe weather conditions. Abuse of pepper spray, kids tossed into walls, heads punched, bodies kicked, and spirits splintered occur with alarming incidence coast-to-coast. And always the rumble of mean words to shatter and destroy a child. A sole occurrence is reprehensible. The magnitude of mistreatment violates not only the United Nations ethos, but every decent heart.

Physical restraints, strip searches, solitary confinement, and corporal punishment summon images of dangerous criminals, not children who have dared to be truant, defiant, or partake in the deeds of youngsters chronicled through the ages. Unquestionably there are those youth who have committed serious and dire offenses, although still minors. Urgently, we must recognize that these kids are not equivalent to adults. They remain children, psychologically and neurologically, as well as socially and emotionally. All deserve protection and humanity as justice is wielded. Rampant maltreatment of youth in any facility, even one, mandates action, reform, and an application of justice to the transgressors. Rehabilitation can never thrive in an environment of cruelty, excessive force and emotional carnage.

Agonizing screams follow the stream of pepper spray. The cries and shouts of children blast into the ears of the bystanders, as measures to alleviate this suffering are called into action, or not.

Science tells us that eyes can suffer lasting damage, respiratory issues ensue for many, and for some, death is possible. Rather than provide positive intervention, chemical restraint can bring a lasting animosity between kids and staff. Severe suffering is inflicted, dropping kids to the ground in wrenching, writhing pain. In spite of "Do Not Spray" lists, kids continue to be sprayed with dire outcomes to health. Occurring across the nation in states that allow pepper spray, canisters are emptied into eyes and faces of children, sometimes with fervor and disregard for those being sprayed. It is an epidemic of cruelty in a culture of disregard for the safety and well-being of children.

Watching a schizophrenic kid, a bipolar kid, or a conduct-disordered kid jailed in the throes of an illness and acute episode prompts an urgent, virtuous concern. One urgent question we must ask, "Where is our humanity?" Then, how can we continue a practice in which jail houses juvenile *patients*? And how can a kid, pushed to the edge of life itself be confined in a 23 hour lockdown setting with an officer constantly watching to make sure a life isn't lost? Who is responsible if that happens? Who is accountable if the check doesn't occur? Ever disturbing, ever frightening, ever haunting, these questions move us to deep reflection, further questions, and finally, to action. And when will the screaming at kids stop? Words bellowed crush hearts and minds, and leave the wounded even more broken.

The system is unconscionably broken and we have an epidemic of kids growing up in shackles and cuffs. Where is Candace now? Where is Christopher? What about Alyssa? She was 12 then, 25 now. Did she survive? Is she drug addicted? In prison? In a grave? I was proud to be her teacher. New to juvenile court school, I struggled daily to find my way to effective teaching and learning while protecting the hearts and spirits of my students. Staff told me daily that it was a miracle that I could keep her in the classroom. The real marvel would be her survival and emergence to a positive adulthood.

There haven't been enough miracles. I have seen kids lost to the trauma and drama of mental illness, conduct disorders, rage, and scholastic poverty. And what about Emily? Incarcerated as a teen, a life sentence for her adulthood, and a multitude of questions loom. Are the children of Candace in juvenile jail now? They would be teens. Very sadly, they could be incarcerated, just like their mama, and their grandma and grandpa.

Over the years I have met many parents, foster parents, grandparents, aunts, uncles, older siblings, and guardians of kids in custody. Many are noble, sitting week after week beside their loved one, delivered in cuffs and sometimes in shackles. Most give heart and soul to the resolution of these immense hurdles before them. These adult visitors are searched, and then wait till their youngster arrives at what is called *Visits*. I have sat face to face with the tears and sobs of these visitors and marvel at their humble efforts to salvage and endure this phase of life with their child. Most often it is the merciless door of poverty that initially creates circumstances of such chronic despair, an often impassable barrier that perpetually prevents the essential opportunities that are vital to children and to childhood.

And others, able to provide the financial and emotional resources that their children need, may find their son or daughter racing down the path of demise called addiction. Brutal and gripping conditions embrace that child who has succumbed to the addictive journey. Seeing their child treated as an offender rather than as a patient evokes immense grief and fear, knowing that retribution instead of treatment follows. A powerlessness ensues, knowing that a system, broken and punitive, will decide if medical care will be provided, if counseling will be offered, or if essential care of any type will arrive in time to address the insurmountable physical and emotional pressures of substance affliction.

When a child is jailed, the entire family becomes incarcerated. The walls of prison extend far beyond the physical display of cells and razor wire. Mothers weep for their sons, care for their grandbabies and even a *baby mama*, and then live a vigil of hope during the days, weeks, months, and sometimes years of a sentence. Grief for a daughter, possibly pregnant or with an infant or toddler at home, becomes a well of anguish and woe. To have childhood stolen by drugs and alcohol, and by the influence of peers already captured by the crime scene, seeds heartbreak.

Sadly, numerous parents have inflicted malice, and others have abandoned their children, resulting in untold suffering. Tragically, many parents cannot show up for their children. They, too, are overwhelmed with the fractures of life, the chaos of poverty, addiction, incarceration, gang affiliation, and mental health strains. It is beyond their scope of living to step up and shepherd their offspring. The generational heritage of a criminal life overrides the instinct to protect, nurture and guide these children. Across the spectrum of hope, most parents seek a safe and decent life for their family, even though those very hopes are dashed by the existence of urban blight, and by a justice system that persists in withholding the full measure of redirection and redemption.

An eminent justice, Judge Marsha Slough, says it takes seven mentors to reverse conditions for an at-risk kid. Where are we? Who are we? Let's show up before it's too late. Some say it already is. I want to believe that an open heart, an ardent spirit, community advocacy, mental health intervention, and strong teaching practices can reverse the ruins of incarcerated parents, drugs, street crime, poverty, and an intergenerational shame that seeds itself life after life after life. My students recycle. I see them as 12-year-olds and soon to be exported to a county jail or adult prison on their 18th birthday. *My children. Your children. The world's children.*

I have learned with utter conviction that I will show up tomorrow with an open heart, steadfast spirit, cutting-edge curriculum, and with compassion, whether in a court school classroom or on the frontline of a juvenile justice forum. Through word and deed, I can foster hope and rebirth. I will listen deeply and teach my kids to do the same. In that exchange of hearing one another, each can reach for the wisdom to walk toward a positive adulthood, attaining a full measure of their potential, and surrendering the agonies of lost childhoods and suffering that define kids in custody. Kids in jail. Life without mercy.

Jane Guttman
California Correctional Educator

Prologue

The child—the child who stands as surrogate for the tens of thousands of children. In the loneliness of the institution, in the darkness, the spotlight comes up and there is the boy or girl who is alone. They wear an orange ill-fitting jumpsuit. Head down, hands clasped in front or perhaps cuffed behind. Orange plastic flip flops on their feet and the light cascades to give detail to the fragile face as it comes up and asks in a small voice that grows in volume. The fragile voice, breaking in its pubescence, begins by asking why they are here. They list the circumstances of being abused, ignored, molested, raped—not knowing where food was coming from, not having enough money for clothing-which is then dirty and smells from an inability to wash—and subsequently bullied by other children. It lists the lack of school programs, the growth of police in the schools, the lack of any expectation of success. The child, the children, speak of the generations of poverty, the depth of poverty, the stigma and weight of poverty that crushes the family system and in turn vanishes the men that could have been productive, lest they have been caught up in the same system, generation after generation. The voice becomes raspy with the stress of a systemic anxiety caused by generations of uncertainty and insecurity. The voice gains strength and resonance and begins to make demands. LISTEN TO ME. Listen to our stories and understand the mitigating circumstances that fostered these actions. Listen to WHY our world virtually demanded these actions to survive.

Then we realize this prologue speaker, is not actor but a very real 10, 11, 12, 13 or 14 year old child and with that there is a silence....the stage goes black and the stories presented here begin to unfold. The prologue can only set the stage—it is up to us as a society to write the epilogue. We are at a unique point where after the nadir of our treatment of these children has been reached, we are slowly climbing out of it and beginning to understand the value of treating these kids with compassion. But it is only the beginning.

The stage is set, the prologue has been presented.....and now it is time to carefully listen to the voices presented with all the attention and humanity we can muster.

Richard Ross
Santa Barbara, California

First Words

It is said that no one really knows a nation until one has been inside its jail.

— Nelson Mandela

JAIL FOR KIDS IS A BIG POT OF TEARS. Street soldiers, once in custody, weep deep into the night, their sorrows stretching into a future that is often bleak and streaked with regret. Hearts bruised from appalling traumas, spirits smashed by betrayal and brutality, now find their way amid shackles and cuffs, searches and more searches. Lost childhoods line the hallways and shade a facility with woe.

The storm of chaos has no season. It rushes into the morning and hovers into evening, giving no reprieve. Even the quiet of night is turbulent, with longings, anguish, tears, fears and fury. The river of rage lurks and is sparked by even a hint of conflict. These soldiers are ever-ready for battle and welcome the stage for fists and even a crafted weapon, saved for the perennial, passionate storm.

Broken lives abound. Rage surfaces without warning, and a stream of suffering floods the space where we hope to open hearts and minds. The trail of anguish goes on and on and on. For kids it is scandalous, tragically scandalous.

The booking cell at juvenile hall houses young offenders with crimes ranging from minor infractions to murder, and as they are moved out to more permanent living quarters, a harsh and an ugly chapter of life begins. A series of traumas commence, from exposed toilets and showers, to long hours in isolation, suicide watches, and the threat of pepper spray and restraint. All this a far cry from what childhood should embody.

Some youth never recover from a lost childhood and related traumas. The bleak burdens of growing up without a true childhood often end in the dark, dead-end of incarceration. Imagine not having parenting, love, food, shelter, and beyond the basics, inspiration and guidance for a secure future. This is the heritage for many kids in custody. Shackles and shouts in the night, door banging, suicide-watches, and fury are universal markers for a juvenile jail sentence throughout our nation. Sometimes the answer to door-banging is pepper-spray, a remedy that will quiet the banging and disarm the banger, distracting the mission to announce his or her anguish and rage. Sometimes a banger starts a banging concert, and many kids join in. The sound is deafening, a chorus of angst and rage from the bowels of juvenile suffering. Eventually the racket is silenced. The hush is a great relief to all those in the general area, and at least for the moment, the routine of juvenile hall resumes and order rules.

After more than a decade of working *inside*, the chaos still seizes me. Anguish prevails. Far too little shields young wards trapped between cement walls and dark despair. Threats of physical and verbal violence create a culture of fear, isolation, and extreme vigilance.

Images of harm flash through my mind with a sting of sadness and a sea of fury. Both as witness and as forager, I have met these harsh moments and disturbing conditions at the hands of those entrusted as *in loco parentis*. The screaming of staff at close-range, face to face with youth, verbal assaults, physical brutalities, shaming and degrading, and the repeated refrain of retribution are far too common. All are appalling, cloaked in the line of duty, yet a sanctioned harm nonetheless — a national crisis and call for reform.

Compassion, humanity, and concern exemplify many probation staffers, even as the relentless spirit of retribution and cruelty thrives among their misguided peers. Finding officers that hold strongly to a belief in rehabilitation has been a long-standing quest for me. Accord, as one by one, their dedication, civility and excellence are discovered, and a worthy partnership ensues for the well-being and humane care of our youth.

In some facilities, the culture of punishment goes far beyond what could be deemed acceptable. The practice of ignoring medical emergencies, ignoring youth in need of protection, and pressing kids past their physical, mental and emotional limits occur in spite of the cadre of ethical officers. Tragic, senseless deaths have ensued, and these losses leave legacies of unbearable emotional scars for loved ones. ⎯

There is no immunity to the collective pain of incarceration. I am never prepared for the story that will be shared when a kid decides to talk about the twists and turns of an impoverished street life without the basics of food, shelter, love and hope; rather growing up with the pain of abuse, neglect, homelessness, poverty, parental absence and emotional adversity. And often, teenage pregnancy.

Imagine a young mother whose newborn lands in NICU after drinking drug-contaminated breast milk, and her screams result in a symphony of generational misery, with a mother and grandmother strongly enmeshed in the prison system. Sadly, this story plays and replays across the nation, and a new generation of at-risk youth is born into conditions that exude despair and disenfranchisement. Even male juveniles do not escape the baby drama, often missing the birth of a first or even second child, or the milestone of a first word or step. Tragic accounts of wretched childhood moments lynch the spirit of innocence of thousands of incarcerated youth in our nation.

And then there is school — including creative writing, a path to salvation for many jailed learners. Students arrive, escorted by correctional officers and a teacher's day begins with the tools of our trade, which include an HT, a radio that will bring help on a moment's notice if rage spills into violence, or a mentally challenged student loses control and becomes unruly, or if the whole room turns into one big brawl. All this is routine and even ordinary for school inside a correctional program, creating undue commotion and grave obstacles to learning.

A hush settles over the classroom as students in jail jumpsuits wait for the next prompt, thankful to leave a lonely cell behind and get lost in science, math, social studies or writing. Students in detention are eager to write. Their stories, waiting to burst like the robin's egg on its final day, defy the grim surroundings and are fueled with new life and its promise. Akin to the budding robin chick, these jailed learners inch through a softening shell as nature has arranged, allowing for the grand possibilities living offers.

Once the invitation goes out for writing time, students sit in anticipation of receiving a journal and a pencil. Something so seemingly routine quickly becomes complex when a pencil needs sharpening, or disappears. Pencil points have to be checked before disposal and all students are closely monitored at the sharpener.

Weapons can easily be crafted from missing pieces, and cutters might embed a point beneath their skin and end up in the clinic or ER, or attack peers or staff with a pencil morphed to sudden shank. These detours to learning are essential aspects of keeping things safe and secure.

Most incarcerated youngsters have never been heard. Some have never unveiled those bitter tales of woe. Once the silence has been broken, some incredible stories surface. Court school can be a raft in high waters, an anchor to lives drifting in dangerous channels, but for many, sadly, school in jail may not lead to the success we seek, despite our best practices. We are always seeking to redirect, educate, and transform.

Watching these young offenders march silently, hands behind their backs, to the step of despair and wrath is chilling. On occasion, a few of these young inmates move with a shuffle, shackled to a well of indignity and struggling to keep their balance, with hands cuffed and chained to their waist, spirits sinking, distraught, but listening to commands with great intent. The sight is gripping, and even after years of watching the scene play and replay, hearts still reel.

Juvenile hall will always be a bleak, cold, tumultuous and painful experience for children, sparking criminals and often, writers. It's a fierce setting in which to generate accomplishment, but we have all seen the weeds emerge between cracks in concrete, trusting the power of seeds to override obstacles of the greatest magnitude. The rose bushes that once lined the walkways have long since disappeared. They vanished in the angst and reverted to ash as all things do. That pretense of beauty has been replaced by the harsh view of bars, barbed wire and razor strips to keep offenders in and outlaws out. Student achievement rises out of the dust of broken dreams and lost childhoods, promising something more, something real, something proud. Their stories become an anchor to hope, a torch for a better tomorrow, a chance finally to be heard, with tales that carry a troubled teen to dignity's shore, giving birth finally to that creative spirit, long buried and now emerging, shackles and all.

The stories that follow, *my portrayal,* my narrative of kids in custody, dignify the magnitude of so many lost lives. In the telling, I honor my wise, bright, wounded, courageous, troubled, creative, and often broken students. *My words* for their heartbreak, their struggles, their tears, stand in tribute to their woes and to their redemption. I marvel that they are still standing after walking the brutal and burning sand of their lives. With my rendition I leap into the fire of truth and trust that my verse will find just the right eyes, ears, and hearts.

Kids in Jail is fictionalized nonfiction—sketches of events that occur inside juvenile halls across America, and although they are told by me, I cannot speak to whether or not these incidents are universal. I believe, however, they are not exceptional, occurring coast to coast in our nation's juvenile facilities. In recounting these events, I have used creative license in an effort to represent them from some of the countless youth who live and endure these conditions. I do this not to *speak for* but rather to give *voice to* them, and to their experiences. The verses that follow are a call to action, a plea for humane justice for a nation of incarcerated children.

I have used the spirit and essence of empathy throughout the pieces that follow—my words for the journeys of kids in custody, intuiting their hopes, dreams, despair and defeat.

Each selection is a composite of many children who have experienced incarceration in our nation. All names are fictitious and the content of the pieces arose from my interpretation of the journey of custody for kids.

Poet Offering

Anytime anyone decides to sit and work with a child who is confined, anytime someone shares the grief and sorrow and joys and laughter with a child who finds herself behind bars, or when a lad makes a mistake and finds himself in a cell and someone comes to see him and they read a poem, when a girl no one has ever cared about turns around to find someone who wants to listen to her poem, well, then, you've got a situation as sweet and rare and so essential to living a full life rich with compassion and empathy, that all one can do, to show one's respect from afar, is bow in reverence to both their souls, and hence, to all souls reaching their true selves through poetry, their true selves, as bountiful and beautiful-filled as a saturday morning sky and a land awash in golden sunlight...

jimmy santiago baca
poet, author

ALLIE

This bitter teen could live her entire life incarcerated, or rise up from the rubble of ruins that has defined her troubled life. Allie understands her assets and she may be determined enough to use them in her quest for a life without bars.

> *I have always found that mercy bears richer fruits than strict justice.*
>
> — Abraham Lincoln

I am a hugger and a screamer.
If you meet me you won't forget.
You'll love me you'll hate me.
But you will not rub out my mark.
I have spent my childhood in this cage.
My tears line the hallway.
My screams locked in the walls,
a record of my pain and woe.

I've sat on this bench year after year
trying to find the part that's whole.
Listening to too much yelling and commands
that make me retch.

I see your hardened hearts
smirking and muttering.
You are stars at disrespect
and I'm learning well.

Thank you for teaching me more about anger
and how to judge and blame,
qualities I'm sure will serve me
in the next step of my captive life.

You met my spirit
that longs to hear the morning bird.
To touch the soft face of a newborn chick
and gather in the smell of roses.

Yes, I really am human
but you don't see it,
while you hammer away
at the scraps of my hope
and pieces of my promise.

Do you know that your words
punch and bite
scorch and sting
stab and scorn,
while my ears long for love?

....

I am strong and I am broken.
I am harsh and I am crushed.
My voice sputters and spits,
choking on venom while
hatred seals my heart.

Juvy is my home
but I don't have shelter.
Walls that punish and puncture.
Today is a curse
that will become yesterday's defeat.

I am tall and I am tough.
A fleeting piece of promise.
A giant with wings of poison
that wrap around a splattered
future going nowhere.

....

Too many sad stories up in here.
One girl cryin' and cryin'
cuz her mama didn't have no food,
stayin' in a motel with all the kids.

Then, guess what?
Teacher met the mama in the parking lot
with a week of groceries.
Not even Christmas,
just groceries.
Goodbye tears.
Then they went to sleep
on a pillow of peace.
The mama and the homie.
One in jail, one at the motel.

Not much peace for me.
Will you pull me back
to a hopeful shore,
toss me a line in my sinking waters,
chase away the demons,
unlock the waiting gift?

Oh I do know that I am smart!
And I could catch the bus to fame
riding in the lane of dignity,
triumph rising from a trench.

I am almost eighteen
time to tell the truth
about how some of you
really do care.

I know it.
I saw Ms. U. stayin' over on her shift.
Not watching the time, just stayin'.

Some special program and she didn't complain.
Then some new staff, real young,
asks our teacher for books.
Wants us to read.
Wants us to succeed.
Wants us to get outta here and stay out.

I fight against admitting it
so I can stay a victim.
Sometimes your caring is real
and I fall asleep with your compassion.

....

There is that big question.
Will I live my life in prison,
a snarling tigress in a twisted jungle
or will I climb to freedom's shore?

My voice booms out.
A drum of anguish
for lost days and bitter nights.
A cold tune of fear but not the finale.
There is more to me
than shackled times and weeping rivers.
I dream of dignity and praising voices
though I walk with a stumbling step.

Take my hand that I might find
a gracious road
that delivers me
to a song of mercy.

RICARDO

Ricardo could live behind bars until death, one of 2,200 kids in the United States who will not be eligible for parole and who may accumulate a lifetime of memories behind barbed wire and among armed guards. Goodbye to mandated education and a juvenile court school. Ricardo could spend long hours each day in a single cell, about 70,000 hours for a sixty-year prison lifetime. Prison conflicts, stabbings, rape and more await. Hello to the perilous life that is prison.

> *I believe in mercy.*
> — Malala Yousafzai

I'm a lifer.
No parole.
That's that.
I messed up.
My teacher asked me am I afraid.
What do ya think.
She said go inside to the well of courage
and live from there.
Not so easy.

Been here since age 15.
Heading to prison soon.
Not sure what's ahead,
just know that I'm scared.
The big house is big.
Knives and shanks and rapes
make me shiver.
Tattoo on my face can start
a big mess.
Just a walking ad for violence.
I'm just a kid.
In book club till then.

Teacher says books are a lifeline.
Takin' me on trips to everywhere.
Teachin' me about livin',
how to build my mind
and find my heart
through stories and glories.

Even some judge came to club
and said she was glad to know us.
Glad to see we are really kids
beneath our soldier steel.

I'm a writer.
I'm a reader.
I'm an artist.
Read at college level.
Have a tattoo on my face.
If you knew me outside
you'd think I was somebody.

I'll send a letter to my teacher
and remind her who I am.
Say, "I'm Ricardo, with the tattoo on my face."
Said she'll remember me.
Said my spirit is staying with her.

I'm gonna cry when I say goodbye to her.
She will too.
She says her heart gets heavy,
real heavy, with all these sad partings.
She's met too many lifers.
That's messed up.

My teacher sees me.
I can tell.
She talks to me like I matter.

Like I'm important.
Like my life counts.
Not that she's okay with my crime
but that's something we can't change,
gotta go on and keep goin' on.

See I didn't know when I was
on the streets that I had gifts.
I didn't know.
I learned about that in book club,
all those stories about gangbangers,
thugs, druggies and then they rose
up out of it.
They got college and jobs
and someone to hold their hands
in the tangles of life.

My life was tangled from birth.
Father dead from drugs.
Mama in and outta prison.
The streets were my *familia*,
givin' me food and shelter
and soldier love.

I was somebody on the street.
Now I'm one of too many kids
serving LWOP in my state.
Life without parole.
Life without mercy.
Not gonna be a teacher,
or a dad or a doctor or firefighter,
or tattoo artist.
Gonna be an inmate.

....

We had this attorney visit
month after month and read
stuff like *Ender's Game* and then
we talked all about it and she said
being with us really mattered to her life.
Really, she said that.
And she isn't a public defender,
she's a district attorney, I mean a *prosecutor*.
And she still came to be with us.

At first one of the kids was very tough on her.
He thought she was scum and messed us up.
We found out *not so*.
We found out.

The judge sent our teacher a box of books
about some dog that told the whole story.
My teacher wanted to check it out first
and sat down at her desk to read it and stayed
there till she finished it.
I had to read it after hearing that.
The judge and the attorney wear nice clothes,
smile hello and smile goodbye and listen to us in between.
They see us as kids, not crimes.
When they walked into max
they brought books, hope and love.

....

One day our teacher showed us
some videos of this girl
who wrote a book and told her grisly story.
We had the book, too, *Runaway Girl*
and found out that her pimp got over 100 years
after he got caught.

Our teacher was amazed
at how much we cared about the author
and her tortured story,
and the word teacher used was *empathy.*
I got a lot of that.
It's when you give your heart.
Really feel it for someone.
Sad to say I won't be having no kids to pass it on to.

....

One of the homies was writing his book in juvy
and all those pages got caught up in a big search.
Tossed in the trash can
and then sent off to the dumpster with no goodbye.
Like about a hundred pages.
I thought the kid would go off,
really off, but he didn't.
Just a short round of door bangin'
and then some deep breaths
till he remembered what his grandma said,
"Don't argue with life."
So he didn't.
Was a proud, juvy soldier on that one.
Teacher's always sayin'
be your best self,
wherever you are.
Those searches are killers.
Take our dignity and our words.

....

One book I won't be forgetting is Anne Frank.
Her diary.
Read it cover to cover, then again.
She had a big street life, then a cell.
Called it an attic.

I cried when I read that she didn't make it.
Innocent, sweet girl, hoping to grow up.
Was counting on her to survive.
No one saw my tears
honoring a distant homie.

Teacher brought a Holocaust survivor out here.
Was a kid during that tragedy.
Listen to this.
He said visiting us was the best.
I mean, he really liked us, cared about us.
Came back 5 times.
Once a year.
Lost his whole family.
Told us about the last goodbye with his daddy.
Some kind of prayer before he got on the bus.

This guy treated us with respect.
Even after some kid raised his hand and said
no such thing as a Holocaust.
Some kid called him an old Jew
on the way to the program.
Anger flashed his face,
took a big breath and
came back the next year.
Heard he died.
RIP dear homie.
Shalom…

I heard about this.
Some kid couldn't come to hear him.
His class was out of control.
He begged to meet the guy.
They made it happen.
He had his audience with the survivor.
They even shook hands.

The kid said he'd teach his grandkids about
the whole thing.
Meetin' a survivor, a Jew.
The kid said was way better
than reading a history book.
Rumor has it there were some tears.

This is pretty sad.
I heard this kid tell our teacher
that he really liked her.
Then he said if he met her on the streets
he might have to kill her.
Since she's Jewish.
Said no room in the world for Jews.
Sad thing, he wasn't kiddin'.
Glad the survivor didn't hear about this.
His heart was already broken by hate.

....

Speakin' of broken hearts.
I'll be in bars and cuffs and searches till my last breath.
Sorry, oh so sorry for my mistake.
It was big.
Really big.
I was a kid when I made it.
Now I'm gonna pay till I die.

I broke a lot of hearts.
Sorry isn't big enough.
Wish I could make it right.
Broken hearts and a sad story.
Mine is broken too.

....

I love book club.
One day my book will be in the club.

A story of tangles and twists,
of loss and pain and triumph.
I won't give up, I just won't.

My words will find hearts.
Crack open minds.
I read the dictionary
in free time.
Another kid, too.
Teacher gave us one
to keep.
Sounds nerdy but
our vocabulary
will catch you.

Some of us, me, too,
are really smart.
Not just street smart.
We won't get a chance
to use that gift.
We're gonna be in
cells and shackles
till the end of time.

Teacher says I can use
my gift anywhere.
Even in prison.
She says there's this prison
debate team that even beat
the team at Harvard.
Some big college in the east.
Says I could be on a team
like that.
Maybe someday.

Hard to believe
about the debate team winning.
Sure gives me hope even so.
Something to dream of,
wish for, strive for.
If I get a chance
I'll sign up.

....

Too many times
club gets interrupted.
A kid messing up.
Time after time, it happens.
All of a sudden
I see lots of staff
in front of a kid's door.
That kid is trouble.

Like the other day
when the kid covered his window.
This is after he stole OC.
Ya know, pepper spray.
He got a cell phone, too.
From a therapist.
Made some calls.
Not sure who, but had the
phone all night long.
Not sure what else he stole.
That kid had a binge.
I think he sprayed staff
or even some kids
and was on lockdown.
Couldn't even believe it.
Like the kid just sprayed away.
Then he got his turn.

It was a shower of spray
with a bunch of burning eyes
and the usual screams,
cuz that stuff is mean.
Everyone coughing and sputtering.

And that's the end of book club
for now cuz the teacher
coughs and sputters
until she walks right outta here.

....

Covering the window of our cell
is a big, big deal.
Every once in a while
somewhere in a juvy, somewhere
a kid or even two is found
hanging in his own cell.

I feel pretty bad for the staff
who finds that mess.
And I lose a piece of my heart for that kid.

Down in Georgia, a kid did it on Easter.
No chocolate eggs and treats, just a
body bag and some tears.
Heard that the kids nearby kept yelling
at staff to help.
No one came.
What's up with that?
Middle of the day.
Where were they?
RIP homeboy.

One time a kid tried to do it with a sock.
They found him in time

24

and the next stop was the psych ward.
Pretty sure he came right back.

I think he was handicapped
and confused.
Didn't know what was happenin'
and where the hell was his helper.
Then the next day
they had counselors for the staff
in case they were bummed out.
I hope they had some counselors
for the kid.

I heard this girl hung herself in California.
Charge was minor.
No big deal.
Here's the big question.
Where was staff?
Really.
Where were they?
Keep asking that question,
but no answers.

I heard out at Rikers
staff beat some kid after
they cut him down.
Hanging on the sprinkler.
Just hanging there.
Then a beating.
Tryin' to understand
all that cruelty.

I even seen cells smothered in crap.
Ya know, feces.
Walls covered, sink covered,
mattress covered.

Like some finger painting
that told the whole story.
Sorry for the kids next to that cell.
A kid tormented and tainted.
And having the last word.

....

One day I was walkin'
to the clinic, late afternoon
and in one of the yards
a group of kids was playin'.
And I wondered about them.
How they got here,
what they want for their lives
and if they would ever get it.

Even though we're above ground here,
even though we have food,
I think we could still drown,
still starve.

....

Club is food for me.
Club is where my heart sings.
Club is where I find me.

Books are my refuge.
Luis Rodriguez,
a big street author
says books
saved him.
Really.

Way back in the day
when he was a young kid,
bangin', he was readin',

even went to the library.
Now he's a famous author,
which I might be one day.

I'm smart enough.
Big question is,
will my words matter.
I think they will.
Pass on my story to the homies.
Tell 'em not to follow my steps.
Not to trash their life,
put down the guns
and go to school.

Listen to this.
This is what my teacher said.
She said I am *her* teacher.
I know what she means.
She means she is better because of me.
So I guess that means my life counts for something.
To make someone else better than before me.

....

Sidney somebody was her teacher
and changed her life.
Now she's changin' mine.

She says she is humbled by our stories.
What does that mean?
I think it means she is so respectful
that she stands in awe of us.
Cuz we walk the burning sand.

She says she won't forget us.
And believe me, I won't be
forgetting her.

When life is very dark
her words can be my light.

She tells us all the good things.
She says she is honored to work with us.
Honored.
I feel taller.
I feel smarter. And braver.
I feel good inside, real good.

She says there's all kinds of wealth.
Then she says she's rich to be with us.
She calls it spirit wealth and tells us
we are her spirit soldiers.

Not sure what that is.
But I feel it.
I feel it in my heart.

We are warriors.
Heart warriors.
Spirit warriors.
On our feet till the last breath.
Standing, still standing.

To R., my beloved student, hoping for mercy in your *life without parole* life.

WILLIAM

William is a heartbreaker. Tragedy has met him at every turn and he longs to be important to even one person. He is a cutter. Suicide has been on his mind. In his anger and in his sorrow, we find the depth in which we have failed him. Betrayed by family, unseen by teachers, William has survived by a slender thread. His life, in the present and in the past, is and was wretched. He is a scar on all of our hearts.

> *You can chain me, you can torture me, you can even destroy this body, but you will never imprison my mind.*
>
> — Mohandas Gandhi

Huddled in my bed
wrapped like a mummy
inside a blanket smellin' like Clorox,
fumes killing the decay in my heart.

You can scream at me.
You can threaten me.
You can shove me.
You can spray me.
You can kick me.
You can starve me.

You can beat me.
You can degrade me.
You can detest me.
You can molest me.
You can do it all.

I don't care.
Oh for one flashing second
I feel the sting of your words and your acts.
Don't worry,

you're not the first.
No one likes me, nobody.
Been that way forever.

Tonight I wail in walls of cement,
secretly, silently,
while the world on the outs
sings and eats cookies
decorated with bright colors
and happy figures.
Holiday angels and snow people
dance across snowy fields.
Whispers of love and surprise
packages, I imagine,
but not in my life.
Just hollerin' staff and the ones
who feel sorry for me and all of us
sittin' in cement, cold and alone.

My foster mom is used to visiting me here
at holiday time, anytime, and her tears
could wash away my fury.
Then I'd have to face my sadness
that pierces my wall of steel,
and feel that mountain of pain,
crushing and cutting me.

A chorus of tears roars,
a symphony of our suffering.

My life has been one long tear
but you won't ever see me cry.
My silent sobs suffocate me,
keep me crouched and stiff
and one step this side of death.

That's right,
I'm dyin' and it's okay with me.
I'll figure out a way,
not today.
And would you even care
or will I vanish into a wave of nothin'?
Will you cry at my grave,
regret your disgust,
feel sorry for my lost life?

No one will ever call me a rising star.
My life just rolls on
with no beat, no tune, no song.

I look around and time just blurs.
Kids millin'
around but going nowhere just like me.
We got pencils in our hands,
quite a story to tell
but no one is listenin'.
Our words just rant,
tellin' a dark story.

This one's dark.
Real dark.
Kid at Rikers.
Out in New York.
In solitary.
Knew he was dying.
Kept cryin' out for help.
Screaming in pain.
Wanted to call his mama to say goodbye.
Died on the floor of his cell.

Another one, too.
Down in Florida.

Kid got beat to death.
By other kids.
Someone said staff gave snacks for the attacks.
Maybe even a Whopper.
I ain't been asked to beat no one.
Not yet.
But I seen mean things in here.

They call it honey bunning.
Staff gives some treats
and the kid does a beat down.
Punches fly and fists find the mark.
The kid in Florida got bunned.
RIP homie.

....

I been watchin' to see if anyone cares.
I see this one and that one
puttin' a piece of kindness into a voice.
Then, one of 'em yells and seems to despise me.
Loser is marked on my face, in their eyes,
I am nothin', nobody.

I gave up on my life way too early.
Don't know how to pick up the pieces
of a shattered me that chokes and sputters.
I can't even remember the last time I laughed
and felt the fun of life, with moments
that didn't have no tears and scowls.

I saw a bunch of kids at a park, gigglin'
with screeches of joy,
some grown-ups even joinin' in.
I don't think that ever happened to me,
to live light and bright and feelin' special
with someone tall and smilin'

reachin' down to pat my head.
Or let words of praise roll out
on a carpet of love.

....

Some of the days get
very dark.
I mean very dark.
So seein', really seein'
is a big effort
that I sometimes can't make
and I crawl way up inside
my own heart and self,
like that's all there is
and then, my tears
crowd out too many thoughts.
When that well goes dry
I'm left with one big lump in my mouth
and some big ideas about slashin' my arms
or slicin' my face.

No one understands the part
where I pick up something sharp
and away I go,
designin' my body with shame and hurt,
with times I can't even remember,
times I can't seem to forget.
So I paint a picture of woe
across the canvas of my body
to silence the racin' words
that say way too much,
and to stop the river of anguish
crushin' me with its wicked waters.
That pain doesn't scare me,
it comforts me in some strange
awful way.

And even though
I can't explain it,
it waits for me
while I do a dance
of survival.

Sometimes I feel a sharp slice of pain
riding through my body on wings of shame,
then, a rush of relief
to feel that throbbing jolt as a sting
cuts across my flesh and I bathe in blood and tears.

Then, there is such a fuss.
Call the Watch.
Call a therapist.
Get help for the wacky kid
who treats his body like a
slice of meat.

Pain is my constant companion.
Awake and asleep it finds me.
I long for relief.
Searchin' for some peace.
Can't remember any other way.
Even though I'm lost,
I hope to be found.

Just so you know —
There is a part of me that feels.
That cares.
That grieves.
That believes.
That I may never find.

SOPHIE

Sophie's rage and grief fill up the world. She cannot accept her mother's limitations and abandonment. A red cloak of anger is her constant companion. Violence is Sophie's salvation. Her fantasies for a decent future dim as she lashes out in a storm of rage and uncontrolled acts. Sophie is a threat to herself and to us. Her crimes hasten entry into the punitive and dark world of juvenile custody and adult prison.

> *The most terrible poverty is loneliness and the*
> *feeling of being unloved.*
> — Mother Teresa

Fourteen
Black
Tall
Thin
Special Ed
Virgin
Only child
No father
Disappearing mother
Thumb sucker
Raised in the hall
Angry
Confused
Bed wetter

Now you know everything
and you know nothing.
Misery is everywhere.
I wake up to a new day
in a cell with a toilet,
but sheets still soaked with

pee and shame,
pee and shame.

Everyone knows I pee myself.
Staff proudly tells the whole world.
My clothes are drenched in urine
every morning.
The girls snicker and scowl
while I cringe and moan inside.

More than once I had to wear
wet clothes all day long.
Staff made me.
Even at school.
I stunk like a toilet.

....

Drama is my middle name,
I find it everywhere.
In my shrieks during the night,
my daytime tears and refusals,
shouts of defiance and anguish
that bring staff running and
chase everyone else away.
Chaos is familiar
like my face in a mirror,
my arm by my side.
Order and quiet disturb me.

But today I am quiet
waiting to meet my new
teacher.
She might like me.
She might see the good part,
help me stop the monsters,
lead me to the me that

could be someone,
could do something.

I heard her smile is a mile long
and she is patient.
So far so good,
I like smiles and patience.

I need someone to like me
love me
hope for me
care about me
guide me
praise me.

The girls don't like me
and they don't keep no secrets.
Teasin'.
Snickerin'.
I mad dog every time I can.
Sometimes I get caught
but I don't care.
I'll punch if I have to,
my fists have saved rage
for 14 years and they're
ready for anyone.

....

My caseworker says I need
anger management.
I got news for her.
No way is there a program
that's gonna fix my anger.
It keeps me going,
helps me live another day.

I do feel sorry for myself.
I want my mama but
she doesn't want me.
Nothing is right because of it.
A long winding streak of pain
follows me everywhere
if I think about it.
And if I don't I start punchin',
kickin' and fightin' my way
through life.

I take a punch or two back,
but no way does this hurt
as much as knowin' that
my mama doesn't want me.
The last girl I hit said my
own mama doesn't even
like me and I wanted to smash
her into pieces but settled for
poppin' her in the face.

There aren't enough punches
or tears to erase the pain
for my mama.
She is a dream and a nightmare.
A story with a frantic ending
that never ends,
while I cry and kick my way
through life.

Tell you the truth,
I did my mama dirty.
Can't change that.
For sure she did the same.
She still my mama, right?
Don't know how to live

without her.
Listen to me, please listen.
Someone's gotta hear me.
Just want my mama.

....

Sometimes I pretend.
I make up stories.
My mama loves me,
thinks about me,
misses me.
She even found a house
that has a room for me
with stuffed toys piled high
and sweet scents calling me
to the kitchen.

She tells her friends
about me,
finds cool clothes,
and asks if I'm okay.

I'm not okay.
Everyone knows
and I get worse
day by day.
Pretty soon
I won't find my way back.

They put me on the nurse's list.
I'm glad.
Someone to talk to
that might listen
and find something to
help the rash that comes
and goes,

paints my arms
with splotches of red and itches.
So then I scratch and bleed,
scratch and bleed.

My grandma says to sit
in the bathtub,
fill it with oatmeal
and soak.
But I don't have no tub
and no oatmeal except
a lump of it on the tray.
Grandma can't even
come to visit,
not anymore.
She's too sick and too tired.

....

Chloe's here with me.
She says to think about
my arms feeling good,
feelin just right,
feelin cool and smooth,
not bumpy and red.

She says to close my eyes
and pretend I'm somewhere
special, and wrap myself
in those thoughts.
Chloe never teases me,
she's not
afraid to let the others see
her kindness.
If I ever had a friend, I want one
like Chloe.
My only friend is my grandma

and my worst fear is that she's dyin'.
Can't make it without her.

What will happen to me?
I wanna be happy.
I wanna be cool.
But I don't know how.

....

Ms. D. talks to me
every morning.
I can count on her.
She doesn't really smile
but she doesn't yell
so I know she likes me.
And that gives me a lift.
Like somebody cares,
and she tells me better
times are ahead
which could be true
cuz today sucks.

When I grow up I'm gonna
have kids
and you can be sure
I'll take care of them.
I won't leave them
and at night I'm gonna
tell them a story
or even two.
I won't kick or punch,
or let hot water fly across a room,
landing on their silky baby skin.
I won't smash my hand into
their sweet faces,
my fist shattering their teeth.

I know I have to go to school,
I just have to.
Ms. D. brought me some books
about careers and one about a CNA.
I could be one.
That way I could buy food and clothes
and things my kids need.
And feel like I could look in the mirror
without feeling shame,
my usual feeling when I think of me.

....

One thing I like about me,
the abstinent thing.
No sex till I'm married.
No std's, a happy husband
when I finally do get married.
And my bible study group will
always be proud of me.
I can have a real wedding night
and wear white if I want.
I know lots of girls with herpes
and one with AIDS.
For sure that can mean death.
Don't wanna die that way.
Not ever gonna happen to me,
my legs are crossed.

Some days are way too hard for me
and I'm red with anger
boiling like a pot of water,
with big popping sounds
that keep me from feelin'
way too sorry for myself.
Cuz life is tougher
than I ever could imagine.

A Portrait of Life Without Mercy

Sometimes a pain cuts through
my heart like a knife mincing
cabbage and pieces of me
lie shredded in a pool of rage and tears.

RYAN

Ryan is bright with a promising future, only limited by his careless crime choices. He is gay, secretly, and is obsessed with the threat of hate crimes and his ability to survive in the midst of widespread cultural hatred. He is clear about where he wants to go, and that includes a college education and even a career working on behalf of gay youth. He is moving closer to trusting his mother with his orientation and ultimately could emerge as a strong voice for gay teen advocacy. He is pensive, tender, and deeply reflective even in the confines of incarceration. And he is afraid.

> *All young people, regardless of sexual orientation or*
> *identity, deserve a safe and supportive environment*
> *in which to achieve their full potential.*
> — Harvey Milk

I have a secret.
Only Freddie knows
and he won't tell a soul.
Mom suspects but pretends
everything is cool.

Now I'm in Juvenile.
This can't be happening.
This could be trouble.
All these boys
and staff that look disapproving,
downright hateful.

The tension is thick,
too much going on
and I gotta stay calm.
Cool, like I fit in.
Not so sure that can happen.

Most everyone knows that gays
really get it in juvy.
Some staff let straight kids into a room,
just to beat a gay kid.
Even call the kids faggots.
Some really do that.

The slurs are all over the place,
gay this, fag that.
So I keep real quiet.
Fights scare me
always have.
Don't get me wrong,
I'm strong
but I'm practical.
I know there's more of them
than me.

Staff looks the other way when
a kid wants to punk me.
So far just words but I know
some really bad tales about
gay punking.

I know some bashing is around the corner,
and no staff to protect me.

Some kid got his head jammed
into a toilet just for being queer.
Staff just watched.
Sometimes a big bloody trail
is left over after a few kids
do some big punching on a gay kid.
I heard all about it.

I heard about a kid who had forced sex
up in adult prison,
with a really big cellmate.
No hope for that kid unless
he gets a new cell.

Grapevine said he had some ruptures.
Right after medical
he got put back in the same cell.
Called him Baby instead of his real name.
The whole thing scares me.
I'm a coward.
In high school they say that's gay.
Since I'm already gay,
I'll just say I'm a coward, a big coward.

Some gay kid up in PA suffered.
Got punched in the eye by a staffer
when he was breaking up a fight.
I heard about it before I got here.

Stories just go on and on.
Some guy, really a girl, got housed
with males instead of females.
Not so good.
Here's how that story goes.
Got beat up, every day.
She got all her bedding and clothes
removed from her cell and staff
opened windows even though it was
snowing.
For sure they didn't like her.
Or him.

That's not all.
Some kid got raped and went to report it,

but staff didn't listen.
I heard the kid got beat with a clothes hanger
and I think for being gay.

Big worry about solitary.
They say it's to protect us.
Don't think so, it's brutal and deadly.
Get stuck in there for weeks or more.
Even years for some.
Kids go crazy, no kidding.
Not enough food, thoughts of dying.
No radio, TV, or books, only despair.
Just time, with demons and darkness.
Way too many suicides.
Survivors have scars forever.

....

I'll get through somehow.
Jail isn't new to me.
Even though Juvenile is.
It's a feeling I live with.
Not being able to really be me.
Or at least the *me* I know I am.

There's a lot going on here.
I'm trying to figure it all out.
It's fast paced
but then those long hours in my cell
bring things to a halt.

This is a crash course in
where not to be.
I sense the danger,
the hatred and suspicion.
You know what I mean,
like you can't catch IT.

Not everyone knows that,
which is the problem,
in fact a very big problem.

I'm looking for some stuff to read,
gay books.
There's this book I read at the public library,
Am I Blue.
Some youth authors wrote some pretty pieces
and some writers weren't even gay,
just wrote gay stuff.
I want to keep reading in here.
Teacher says she'll look.
I told her to go to GayYA!
Takes forever to get gay kids gay books.
Staff must be afraid to let us read.

I think human nature
fears what it doesn't understand
and then it takes that fear and turns
it into mean times and dirty deals.
Real dirty.
Even death.

....

Still crying over Matthew Shepherd
and half the world
doesn't even know
who he is.
Still hear his dad's words in my ears,
talking at court about his son,
and how much he loved Matthew.
He said, *Matthew didn't die alone*
in that field, no
he died with the stars and the moon,
with the wind and with God.

49

Oh, how sad for that sweet boy.
So many hearts broken from hate.

I read that speech Dennis Shephard
gave, over and over and over.
Matthew was his father's hero, and
he bowed to Matthew out of respect
and just to honor him.
Now that's a rare moment to share,
father and son.
I can only imagine how Matthew felt,
feeling his father's deepest regard.
That might have been right before
the hate crime.

I heard that Matthew's grandpa died
right after Matthew,
just a few weeks after.
I might be a dreamer
but I see Matthew and his grandpa
together,
sitting in heaven on a cloud of love.

Who even knows,
maybe there's some plan
that some of us die at the same time
to be together, so we feel
like we're with family,
and feel safe and comfort
in a strange time.
I feel peace that they're together.
Hope Dennis and Judy feel that too.

I wonder what my father would
say about me,
if I died tied to some post,

my life cut short with hate
and cruelty, and even ignorance.
I don't think my father or mother
would ever bow to me
or call me their hero.
Not even after I was killed.
Not that they don't love me.
Matthew was more special
than me.

I didn't even have a name
for the first six months.
They couldn't decide,
and then my mom
met this kid in a juice bar
and asked his name.
So then they called me Ryan.
The kid was tall and cute
and wouldn't it be something
if he was gay.

My teacher cries
when she tells us about Matthew.
I mean she doesn't out and out sob,
but I saw the tears gather up in her eyes,
and she takes a deep breath.
Then tells us that hate is always pain.

....

I don't want to die.
Life sits before me
like a prized canvas
waiting for the colors of my life
to spill into some magnificent form,
with bright colors for my joy and feats
and darker ones for my tears.

The numbers aren't on my side.
I read on some tolerance site
that over 60% of high school kids
are threatened, that's gay kids.
I am only 16 and I already know
some guys who died of AIDS
and some who have had their heads
bashed in for being gay.

Matthew was attacked two times
before the one that killed him.
He kept on being who he was
and didn't hide or pretend.
I call that major courage,
just standing up for himself.
One small, brave giant.

Someone broke his jaw
but not his spirit.
I will remember him
when life shows its ugly ways.
He'll be a torch of goodness
when I walk along side of hate.

....

The future frightens me,
mostly about will I have one.
I need to get out of here,
make sure I don't come back.
I have so many questions.
Like can I have a family?
Do I even want kids,
and if I do can I really be a *dad?*

I know a kid with two moms.
No one with two dads.

The kid is kinda proud.
One's the bio mom
with the other one's egg.
So I guess that means two bio moms.
Doesn't act ashamed.
Like he's happy to be their son.

My mom wants grandkids,
but would my kids really be
her grandkids.
I don't know if she would even think so.
I know Dennis Shephard would love
Matthew's children, if that had happened.
Those kids would have lifted
his heart to the moon.

There's so much to think about,
and I'm in the right place for thinking.
I have to watch my back, day and night
since hate can slip through these steel doors.

Hate is everywhere if you're gay.
It hides even in safe places.
So that means no place is really safe.

I used to laugh when kids think gay is contagious,
now I get real serious cuz I know they could kill me or hurt me with
those thoughts.
My brother would die a thousand times
if he knew I was gay.
A chip off the old block, my dad too.
They would think of all those times
we went camping and took those showers
in the park's community shower
like naked is a big deal.

See, gay isn't bad.
And gay isn't sick.
And gay isn't dirty.
And gay isn't you,
it's me
and I'm okay,
at least today.

My crime isn't serious
but very stupid.
Juvenile will be
forever put to rest
in three weeks
when I go home.

I'm heading to CC,
Community college
for liberal studies.
I come from a long line
of folks who are college educated,
and that's a chain I won't break.

After college I might even
work with gay kids,
in some counseling program
that offers guidance and support
about how to grow up gay
and survive.
More than survive, really live.
How to walk down the street
in any neighborhood and make it
without some violent voices
and threatening gestures.
And even death.

Guess I could even work in Juvenile.
Be a counselor *inside*.
Help kids, gay or not.
Be a light in such a dark place.
The brutal stuff has to stop.
Here's what I want to do.
Help kids to feel more than okay,
even proud to just be who they are.
And not to live with that gripping fear
that steals life.

....

I went to a gay parade once,
and didn't tell my parents.
I stood on the curbside in shock
to see all these people,
walking down the street
dressed in all kinds of amazing outfits.
Then the group of professionals,
and I do mean professionals,
nurses, teachers, police people,
firemen and firewomen
walking with signs and placards,
and then all that clapping for them
on the sidelines.

I looked around to see families,
mothers and fathers I assume,
even grandparents,
just there.
Hanging out with gay family.
Like a celebration.
Love and respect and joy.
I was stunned by the whole thing,
like for that moment it was all okay.

The last group was PFLAG,
those parents and friends of
gays and lesbians.
Some moms and even a dad or two.
Gay kids growing up with parents
and they know the kid is gay.
I'm dancing to that!
Since that day, about a year ago,
I've been imagining my mother
in that line, smiling and waving
in support of her son.

JORGE

Jorge is ready to live life and ready to enter the adult world with a plan that has honor. He is learning to make peace with his past and embrace his future. Jorge knows that he must have mentors and he will find them. Compassion and palpable dreams rise from his heart and spirit. Prison is not on his life agenda.

> *You are not defined by your past. You are prepared by your past.*
>
> — Unknown

When I get outta here
headin' to the Navy.
For reals.
Don't talk much about it.
Is a big dream.
Teacher says gotta have a dream.

Gonna be 18 soon.
Not comin' back.
No big house for me, either.
Sayin' goodbye to trouble.
To sounds of my brothers cryin'.
Shoutin' and fightin'.
To cells and sorrows.
To shackles and solitary.
To searches and shame.

I got some pluses on my side.
Speak 2 languages.
Teacher says read in both.
Write in both.
Stay fluent.
Gonna do it.
Wrote this poem

La vida que vivo.
The life that I live.
Teacher memorized it.
Even though she doesn't speak Spanish.
Said it's a winner.
Said I'm a poet.
Said she's keeping that one.
Has a heart library for poems.
Not sure how that works.
Just think it means we can save
something good and see it again
just from remembering.

Then she recited a poem she
learned in middle school.
So I guess the poem library is real.
Not dissin' her but she's old.
Real old.

Lots of time to write in here.
Read.
Am a good reader.
Read hours and hours up in here.
Could teach someone how to read.
Teacher says if you got a gift,
use it.
Don't save it.
Don't waste it.
Use it.

Said if you got a gift,
it's a privilege.
And a responsibility.
Don't leave it on a shelf
to get dusty and stale.
Live it.

Share it.
Love it.

Wanna start a tutor program in here.
For peers.
Help a brother step up to his gift.
Teacher says we all have one.
Some of us didn't find ours yet.

Pretty good at writin'.
Poetry is my thing.
I keep a journal.
Back in the day had
a staff that was big on poems.
Even had a program.

That staff was *bad.*
Ya know.
Bad means *good.*
Real good.
Read all the poetry.
Taught kids how to do it.
Said the way you practice
is how you'll perform.
Just like life.

Gave respect.
I mean like the homies were somebody.
Looked right at us when he talked.
Kids lined up to read their poems
while he sat on a table.
Like a dad, who was lovin' on his kids.

The day always started when he arrived.
Like we knew, really knew
he wanted us to get out of here,

grow up with a real childhood
and do something big in life.

Said he messed up back in the day.
Climbed up out of it.
Got educated.
Chose a job to help kids like him.
I heard he died.
Not expected.
Just died.
Not even that old.

Kids cried when they found out.
Teacher lost someone real important.
Told us he was her hero.
He loved words as much as she does.
That guy was loved.
Respected.
They even named some building after him.
RIP Big Homie.

There's a really cool staff here now.
He loves us.
When that guy walks on our unit,
we all have an inside smile.
Don't show it, but feel it.
Happy, so happy to see him.
Just know the day's gonna be better.
Listen to this.
Some kid was on admin seg
and this staff came by to visit.
Just visit.
On his own time.
Read the kid poetry.
Talked to him.
Asked all kinds of big questions.

Said the kid could do something good.
Something important.
Told the kid he was really smart.

I heard all about it after the kid came back.
He was kinda proud.
Said nice to be seen.
Nice to be loved.
Have someone believe in him.
Liked all that attention.
Kids do.

Gotta admit,
feels good to have someone care.
Need that from time to time.
Like some of the homies in here
ask for a copy of my poem.
Kinda feel important.
One kid asked if he could send it to family.
Teacher asks if I want to read it to the class.
Then everyone snaps their fingers.
Like clapping, but not noisy.
Was nervous at first.
But now I stand up and just start reading.
Get better and better at it.

Poetry's food for me.
Fills me all the way up.
Those words talk right to my heart.
I get lost in their power and peace.
Loved poetry since I was in 6th grade.
Even wrote some birthday poems for my sis.

She's a vegetarian.
Since she was 15.
Said she saw some video

about a 3 year old kid.
Didn't know that meat came from animals.
When he found out, he stopped eating it.
Hard to be a vegetarian in here.

One kid stopped eating meat.
Got real skinny
before they figured out what to give him.
Didn't complain.
Took it like a man.
Wow, was he hungry.
Didn't eat no eggs or cheese.
Guess that's called vegan.
I like burgers.
And cheese sandwiches,
and scrambled eggs.
And ice cream.
So no vegan for me.

Wonder if he'll keep goin' with it.
Not sure.
Some religious thing.
Buddhist, maybe, or Adventist.
Will say this.
Staff was no big help.
Kid was a broken record asking for food
after a while.

Some kid had a scary story
about staff taking away food
when kids talked too much.
Then he said if they took too long
to eat, food got thrown away.
I heard that in solitary you don't
get much and kids beg for food.
Beg since they're starvin'.

Word I think of is mean.
Separated from family,
from homies, from our street,
and then food trouble.
Yeah, I call it *mean*.
Might write a poem about it.

Send it to a contest when I get out.
Could even win a prize.
A money prize.
Get published.
Teacher got her first poem published
in high school.
In some big book.
Some famous guy wrote to her about it.
Very cool.
Maybe something like that's ahead for me.

Wanna fill my head with hope.
Helps drown out some of the stuff
goin' down here.
Too many fights.
And staff with big voices
when quiet would work better.
Wanna hear words that give me hope.
Tired of livin' in the punishment pot.
Just wanna do my program
and go home.

Asked teacher to write a letter for court.
She said *yes*.
Got a good judge and a good teacher.
Showed me the letter, said I could keep it.
Wanna show it to my mama.
Said all these things.
My good traits.

That letter was one long page of respect.
Every word.
Gonna try to be that person she wrote about.
Me, the real me, I suppose.
Without the streets, the homies and drugs.
Said she knew I could get to my goal with help.
The judge agreed.
Gonna get some help.
Keep my dream alive.
Be a sailor.
Have a family.

When the lights go out in here.
I do the Navy salute.
See what it's like.
I stand really tall and proud.
Light up the cell with my dream.
First a GED.
Then the Navy.
Eight weeks of boot camp
and then servin' my country.
Teacher says one step at a time.
Reaching a dream takes dedication and courage.
I got both.

Saw this video in class about Navy recruits.
Listened to every word.
Males and females
sayin' a piece of their story.
Didn't do nothin' good till now,
this kid and that kid, all
sayin' signin' up was the best ever.
Teacher says now is what matters.
That's what we have.
The past is the past.
Learn from it.

A Portrait of Life Without Mercy

Lay it to rest and move on.
Do it now.
Am gonna.

Steppin' up to life.
Doin' something good for me
and for someone else.
Goin' from homie to sailor.
May even end up a POW or MIA.
Or come home in a coffin.
Okay with me, to die with respect.
Draped in a flag with honor.
My mama would be proud.
Pretty sure the homies would be too.
No street death for me.

Read about a special custom.
The Navy leaves an empty place
for a lost sailor at special events.
Round table for unending respect.
Salt on the bread plate for tears.
Red rose for love.

Wow, all this for me if I'm missing or captured.
Lemon for the bitter fate.
Yellow candle for hope that I'll be found.
Just gotta get to boot camp.
Start my life right there.
Then, graduation with family and applause.
A moment to remember forever.
Standin' proud.
Gonna like the title Seaman
with my name.
Man in white.

RASHAD

The future has never looked bright to Rashad. His life has been about survival, having enough food, figuring out the next step, watching his mother's anguish over poverty and her husband's infidelities. And then his disappearance. Not much was left for Rashad, no nurturing, no guidance, and no real hope. Somehow, he knew to reach out to teachers and even a minister for help and hope. There is a chance that he will come to higher places and raise himself out of the chaos and danger of his present life.

> *Life is not about how many times you fall down,*
> *but about how many times you get up.*
>
> — Jaime Escalante

Today's my birthday,
older not wiser,
just a kid
doing grown-up things,
dreamin' 'bout gang signs
awake and asleep
gotta feel like I belong,
be important
follow in my daddy's footsteps,
make him proud.

I've been outta juvy for 3 days.
Can't say I'm sorry to leave that pit
but I do miss the meals, 3 squares.
Not much happening in my kitchen
but stale stuff and empty cabinets.
Mama been laid off and daddy ran off.
He'll be back, just like last time.

We're gonna have a new kid here soon.
Yeah, my cousin's, and I'm glad she lives here,

her house is hell.
Screamin' and fightin' all day, all night.
I told her we'll find what she needs for the kid.
Down by the church there's an old thrift shop.
If they don't give us a good price we'll take it.
Just gotta.

I saw some ads on TV about babies.
So I said no alcohol, no drugs, no, no.
And get to a doctor or else.

....

My mama's scared
I know.
Worried about the baby, not much money.
Nothing saved.
Big burden to make it all work.

Been thinkin' bout gettin' a job.
Ya know, helpin' out.
Buyin' some stuff for the kid,
formula and diapers.
Jonny sells drugs and makes a heap.
I could if I want,
sure ticket back to juvy.
I'm not going back, no way.
Mr. R. says it's not for me.
Says I could do some good things
in my life, and ya know what,
I believe him.

I want more than this.
Oh that teacher always tellin' me
it's up to you.
Yeah, could be true,
I can make a plan,

talk to that place where
kids give up gangs.
The line isn't long there
and I don't have to tell nobody.
Just do it.
Yeah, take that first step like the reverend says.

I know a kid who did that.
Made it out.
But what would I do?
Where could I live?
Gotta change neighborhoods.
New school.
This could get so hard
and real scary.
Yeah, I'm afraid.
That old guy at the store says do it anyway.
No matter how scared you are
God'll help, well maybe that's true.

Teacher keeps tellin' us about a kid,
now a man, that is out.
Wanted to take his kid to Disneyland
instead of to the prison visit room.
Or to a cemetery.

I could roll with that.
Then there's another guy
that keeps coming up in here
to talk to us about how he did it.

Held his baby in his arms
and that was that.
Goodbye gang.
Goodbye crime.
Goodbye drugs.

I don't think it's that simple.
But now his kid's in college.
Can be done.
It can be.

....

And what about me.
Can I have that kind of courage.
Can I walk out of my hood just like that.
Have a big dream,
make it?
Reverend says be brave.

I know the homies
feel good but that doesn't
mean they are good.
I wonder who I am
without the streets.

Read *Yummy.*
Last days of a southside shorty.
All the homies want to read it.

Story of Robert, called *Yummy.*
Loved sweets.
Tough life.
Electric cord scars on his body.
Burn scars by age 2.
And 49 scars at his autopsy.
Only 11 years old then.

Killed some girl in his hood by accident.
Name was Shavon.
Went to church with her.
Shots all over the hood.
Hid for 3 days and then got smoked.

Get this—by his own gang.
Execution style.
Knew too much.
Just marched that little kid
into a tunnel, down on his knees
and then a trip right out of here.

Had 23 felonies by age 11.
Could make the *Guiness* book for crimes.
Got beat up at juvy for his stuffed toy.
Carrying it around like a kid, sleeping with it.
Part kid, part thug.
That could be anyone in here.
Most of us thugs,
all of us kids.

All these adults, even some Prez named Clinton
thought this was messed up.
Tore down the projects,
started programs.
Thought Yummy's death was a big deal.
Teacher was shook up by the story.
Here's what we told her.
Just life for us.
Just life.

Teacher says the killers could be released soon.
Both got GED's and do good in prison.
Want to move on from gangs.
Want to live each day and do good.
Sorry for what they did.
Real sorry.

Saw 'em on a video.
They said no help from the homies.
No letters, no money, no visits, nothin'.

Smoked *Yummy* or they would die.
Now they know better.
Took 'em their whole life to know better.

I just know with my whole heart
that where I am is nowhere.
If I finish high school I'll be the first in my family.
Believe me, would be the first.
Imagine that.
Cap and gown.
Movin' that tassle over.
Holdin' the paper.
Maybe some cheering.
Smilin' and feelin' proud.
Real proud.
My family would fill up the bleachers
at graduation, with their joy and pride,
no doubt.

Some kid in juvy graduated.
Had some ceremony
with cake and punch.
Even a cap and gown.
Family came and gave a speech.

Another kid too.
No family.
Just didn't show up.
He still was proud.
Real proud.

Teachers came and even staff.
Said all these good words,
no pictures allowed to remember
the glory of it all.

Those tough gang bangers
cried when they got that diploma.
Cried, they really did.
Tears of pride,
then weeping for their lost childhood
among the bars and shackles.

MATTHEW

Matthew is remorseful and frightened. His privileged life took an abrupt turn with a choice that could have dire penalties. Life in juvenile hall shocks him and defies any resemblance to his affluent world. Matthew is learning about regret. His life swerves and shakes from his cell, and the future may be irrevocably changed. Matthew discovers what ethics are all about as he struggles with his self-imposed isolation and realization of the severity of his crime.

> *Out of suffering have emerged the strongest souls;*
> *the most massive characters are seared with scars.*
> — Khalil Gibran

I must be in the wrong place.
No way is this for me.
I spent my last summer at the shore,
surfing, playing, a real beach bum,
and now this.

My dad said summer would be a trip to Europe
and time in our beach house.
But some chick spilled things
and said something about a date rape
so here I am.
I can say for sure that I'm sorry,
but it's a little late for that.

My father is furious and my mother
is , well, hysterical.
Disgrace. That's it, she is disgraced.
Like I brought this whole thing down
to ruin their lives or something.

I can't believe the showers.
No privacy, no decent soap

nothing like home.
I've showered in the best,
lathering with luxury
wrap-around towels,
giant terry robes.

This place is bad.
Really bad.
There's a lot of yelling,
kids miserable
and me, shocked at the food.
The accommodations stink.
I really can't eat the food.
You can tell no one knows nutrition
or cares about our health.
My mother reads labels
and wouldn't give this to our dog.
No one here knows about low carb eating
or fresh vegetables.
I bet the peanut butter is hydrogenated.
Come to juvy and get cancer!
That'd make a good billboard.

The bathroom scene is awful.
Appointment only or "head calls" with the group.
Some kids hang up their sheets
like a curtain to get a minute of privacy.
"Sit downs" when you need them,
get used to waiting.
At home, I have my own bathroom.
A real cool one.
I can close the door, take my time
and wash with pricey soap from the specialty shop.

....

One kid on the unit
has pretty big issues
and not enough soap.
Washes his hands till they bleed.
Always asking the teacher,
"Can I use the sink to wash."
She says *yes* every time.
The kid must be miserable.
Just like that guy Howie on TV
who washes and washes and washes.

School is another story.
The teachers are cool.
Dedicated up the kazoo.
But the kids are different.
That's it, different.
You can just tell.
Some actually like it here.
I hear the talk, about having meals,
a place to sleep, a routine.

I heard a couple of kids
say they are homeless.
Said it was good to get off the streets
and have some food.
They have sad stories.
Really sad.
Parents in jail
not much money.

I know they never stayed at a hotel.
Room service, fancy clothes, all of it.
I don't have much to do with them
and they think I'm pretty weird.
Wouldn't mind hanging out,
I mean, in here.

Get to know each other.
Different worlds, but we're all locked up.

Mine is a whole lot easier.
Food and money really matter.
Can't even imagine life without a bed,
or utilities, or regular meals.
I'm getting a real education in here.
All about gangs and drugs and one kid
pulled off a sneaky check scam.
Like that guy, Frank somebody.
The guy who passed all those bad checks.
Now he works for the FBI and is legal.
There's a book and a movie.
Told the whole story.
The title is catchy.
Catch Me If You Can.
The book's in the library.

....

Rachel, that's my sister,
wants to know what I learned.
Wow, I could write a book about it.
Maybe I will.
Title could be
From Jail to Yale.
Yeah, I want to change.
She wants to know what I know.
Mostly that getting caught is a drag
and the consequences are tough.
My charges are really serious.
I read about that kid who's doing 10 years.

Some other kid did something
similar and he's being tried in adult court.
Bad deal, very bad deal.

He might get a long time.
And he's fillin' my head with lots of worry,
like about what's gonna happen when we hit prison,
I mean inmate karma for our crimes.

Kids for sure don't belong in adult jails.
Or prisons.
We all know what happens.
Like throwing a lamb to the lions.
Here's the word that comes to mind.
Savage, it's savage.
Kids are just that, kids, *not* adults.
Another word that works is heinous.
I'm good with words.
Big vocabulary.
Good at spelling.
Hope college is right in front of me.
Not prison.
I want knowledge not violence.
Want to cross rape out of my vocabulary
and do something good for the victim.

I heard about this kid that was raped
when he was a kid, a little kid.
Like about age 6.
He was messed up,
felt dirty and no good.
Looked down when he told me.
No gender is safe from rape in this world.
Two big words come up to my mind.
Remorse and regret,
both can take us all to a new start.

Visits are tonight but I don't want to see my dad.
He's really pissed and doesn't care who sees.
I know my mom won't show,

she can't deal with this place.
She fainted when she heard what happened.
A lot of drama on visit night.
Kids crying, parents crying,
I like when it's over.

No one in my family's ever been here.
My future's pretty scary right now.
I don't really think about missing things,
but I do miss people.
My parents, sisters, and friends.
This is a lonely place.
A lot of people, but no love.

Sometimes people wonder about remorse.
I feel it.
One of the chaplains asked a tough question.
What if that had happened to my sister?
I would be crazy with rage.
Furious.
Sad, too,
that my sister had to feel pain and shame.
One question and my world turned around.
I saw what I did from a different view.

I heard Dr. Phil talk about forgiveness.
Tall order for me.
Working on it.
Trying to find peace in the pain.
Looking for a way to start over.
When I get out I want to help
kids stay away from jail.
I'll ask my dad to help.
Use our money for something big.
First thing I want to do is say
sorry to everyone I hurt in all this.

Everyone.
See how I can give back.
What I can do to make it right.
Start a program.
Turn it around.
Do something about all this pain inside.
Hurting someone really hurts.

Strands of sadness roll over me,
feels like a ton of bricks crushing me.
My breath raspy and labored,
and beneath those struggling breaths,
a sea of tears.

SONNY

Sonny is tormented by his loneliness, craves friendship and love. He asks for little from his family, and that seems too much. He is a poet and has been belittled by all for his bookish ways. His shyness creeps into every moment of his life, yet he is easily inflamed. Sonny's aggression scatters any hope of friendship and connection. He is a captive of the isolation and despair born of that aloneness. He dreams of carnage. His raging threats chill us all.

> *I was kind of a weird homey. I was a weird kid. No one in my family loved books. I was the only one. […] Books saved me.*
> — Luis J. Rodriguez

Call me Sonny.
My shyness has a capital S.
And I cringe.
Wanting to crumble
if you notice me.
And suffer if you don't.

Too much yelling here.
Just like home but scary.
I like quiet.
I like space.
I'm a loner.
Not by choice.

My long hair is *me*.
Wear it pulled back in here.
Gonna get cornrows
when I get out.
Not allowed in here.
My nerdy ways
trigger cruelty from the others.

Everywhere I go.
I hear the words.
They all say
loser.

I really gotta watch my back.
Heard that staff turns away
and lets kids punch away.
I been workin' hard at followin'
what they say.
Don't piss 'em off.
Show respect.
Follow the rules.
Don't want to be the target
of some staff's hit.
It happens.
Heard all about it.
Win-win for the punchers and staff.
Big lose for me.

....

I had a friend once,
when I was seven.
That's what I need.
Now my friends are poetry,
books, trips on the Internet
and too much silence.

Tryin' to get used to things here.
Believe me, that's not easy.
Some kid keeps cryin'
and what a story he has.
When he got here staff
tried to reach his parents
and guess what?

A Portrait of Life Without Mercy

They moved and didn't leave
no address.
Just left the kid.
Moved on.

I saw the look on my teacher's face.
She tried to hide it but that one hurt.
The kid is pretty messed up.
Not knowing where he'll go
or what happens next.

I think the crime was big,
like arson, tryin' to burn down the house.
Well he fixed things, cuz now he's not going home.

Tryin' to figure out how he feels.
Parents leaving just like that.
My mama left that way.
Gave me to some family, now I'm adopted.
Empty place in my heart.
Maybe mama's too.

One day we might look at each other.
Mama and me.
A day I want more than anything.
Maybe we have the same smile,
same anything,
even rage.

The kid got a bum deal
with his folks,
and he's not even adopted.
The guys are listenin' to him cry and whine
but no one's complainin'.

....

I used to cry and whine.
But those days are history.

Red angry dust settles on my life.
I've been thinking about making my mark.

One kid in here is pretty scary.
He's got the red angry dust too.
The teacher is scared.
She tries not to show it, but I know.
I watch her watch the kid and be ready.
Ready for anything.
I saw some teacher in another class,
was watching from my cell.
Teaching her this move and that move,
to defend herself just in case.

Tell you this,
heaven help the kid
that touches that teacher.
We got her back.
Here's why,
she always has ours.

Not sure what the next step is.
Have some pretty dark scenes
in my mind.
Hurtin' everyone.

Nature helps me out.
I've grown tall and strong.
In spite of being a freak.
Don't be walking by me with a look
or my foot'll catch you
as I smirk to your fall.
Not happy about doing it,
but gotta.

Not my fault that I'm smart.
Shouldn't really separate me
from every kid I've ever known.
Well, mostly.

I could teach you things.
Share what I have and what I know.
Like I think friends could do.
I have been outside of every gig.
Watching from the sidelines,
as the world rushes by.
Waiting for a sign
that would let me in.

My cell is a budding factory.
I am creating a scene in my mind
to force your pain.
Since I can't get friendship,
I want you to hurt like I do.
Just want to belong.
To feel okay.
Feelin' real lonely.
Me against the world.

THURSDAY

Thursday's spirit sustains her. The dark spaces of her life fade and she lines up with her power and clarity. She has seen hard times and ugly moments. Her heart is tender as she grieves her sister's pain and struggles to make sense of her father's cruelty. Thursday is hope for kids in custody. Her name lifts the burden of incarceration. She is Thursday's child, and has far to go. She is open to her future, and recognizes drug use as a demon. The mystery of life intrigues her and gives her sustenance. Thursday *does* have far to go and she will get there. We will see her in a college classroom or with a career in education. Her steps are unfaltering; her hesitancy for life disappears into her noble dreams.

> *There is no greater agony than bearing an untold story inside you.*
>
> — Maya Angelou

I love my name,
not everyone does
but it suits me,
ya know, that poem
about days and all.

Monday's child is fair of face,
Tuesday's child is full of grace,
Wednesday's child is full of woe,
Thursday's child has far to go.

That's me, a long way to go,
but I'm ready.
Been reading stuff about tough times
and how they make us grow and grow.
Become strong and wise,
turn things around.
I have to do it.

I believe, I really do,
about things that happen for a reason,
take us to a higher road or something like that.

Watchin' all these girls cry and suffer,
talk about being *back here* over and over,
not me, no way.
This is it for me,
out of here for good when I go.
You'll find me
in gang class or drug class or
how to fix your life class
cuz I have far to go.

Lots of broken kids here.
Lost childhoods.
So many girls with a big street life.
Call it prostitution,
but we know the truth.
It's trafficking.
Brutal to live it and remember it.

Or, sad home stuff.
No mama, no daddy.
Growin' up with drugs instead of groceries.
Refrigerator's empty
and so is the money jar.
Bunch of kids cryin' for food,
and a mama that dodges punches,
even in jail.

I know this kid who has 16
relatives in prison.
She told us in class and asked
the teacher how she could have a chance.
Teacher said "You do."

You turn it all around.
Be the first.
Get educated.
Get a job.
Get a village.
You can do it.
I think she listened.
But I watched her face
and her eyes showed the doubt.
All that family in jail is a lot of woe.

....

Wednesday's child is full of woe,
a poison with tears,
and believe me, there's a flood
of tears here.

My teacher tells us that
we all have far to go.
She says we can do anything
if we decide to.
She says it can happen.
Says it's a gift in the wings.
Not sure about some of the girls.
It might take a miracle.

Like Annie.
She's gonna do time, 25 to *life*.
She's really book smart, not street smart.
Crime was horrid.
Don't even want to tell.
She whispered it to me at free time.
All she wants is to go home.
Her mama and daddy want that.
Not gonna happen.

She's only 14.
Wow, she could do 70 years.
I feel a tear sliding down my face
to take that in.
So many messed up lives.

Like Caren.
She already has two kids.
One at 12 and one at 15.
How is she going to make it?
Her dad is raising the kids.
I think her mom's in jail.
Caren doesn't like the teacher
and she isn't quiet about it.
She has a heart of steel.
Slammin' books around and cussin'.

The teacher tells her to get
her education.
Be a graduate.
Show your kids who you are.
Step up to your best self.
Get your kin to help.

Sorry for her kids.
They didn't ask for all this drama.
Innocent, struggling, no childhood.
Wish life was sweet for them.

Life ain't been sweet,
not yet.
I like that word *yet.*
cuz it gives me hope.
Lets me think about better times ahead,
and to halt my tears for shattered times.
Mostly at home.

A Portrait of Life Without Mercy

Too much arguing.
My dad wasn't cool,
collected other women,
broke my mom's heart,
and crossed that line with my sister.

Something I try never to think about
but it finds me in my dreams
and in those shadows of getting awake.
A sad story, a mean story, an unforgiving story.
We all feel that way
while he's in jail and my sister weeps.

Drugs cut the pain,
a pill here a smoke there.
No needles but I love the high.
Free from pain,
free from reality,
free from too many sorrows.
I can't even count how many
in my almost eighteen years of living.

My mama says stop counting sorrows.
Count blessings.
Just start with one,
then keep going.
You'll make it to one hundred.
One hundred blessings.
She says that's the key to living
and how she keeps her head up.
How she finds the pot of gold
with the rainbow.
How she lets her sorrows
melt into golden threads of goodness
found through the song of her heart
and the beat of those one hundred blessings.

ANGEL

A tough but tender boy, raised in the world of street life and holding fast to his hopes for a future with Lola and their baby, but struggling to let go of his homeboys and the glitter of gang life. Angel is kind and strong, and ready for life's mystery and glory. His mother stands beside him; her hopes for him to reach for the high road are persistent and enduring.

> *We draw our strength from the very despair we are forced to live. We shall endure.*
> — Caesar Chavez

Not again,
back here again.
Strip search,
kids yelling,
crying
and acting crazy.
I won't be in
holding long.

They'll send me to
A maybe D,
either way I
know the ropes.
Same old story.
A bunch of smelly
kids with anger issues
and big fists plastered
behind backs to keep
us safe.

A long walk down
the path in my pajamas
carrying my sheets

and watching barbed
wire meet the night.
Then another search.

Everytime I move
there's another search,
so I just daydream out
of myself while I follow
directions.

Clothes off
lift this, spread that,
cough, cough, cough
nothing found
nothing lost
but one piece of
my pride and
I crawl back into
my skin through
layers of shame.

Lookin' for drugs or weapons.
Like a razor blade taped to a foot
or drugs in an arm pit.
Much harder for females.
The search is rough.
Lots of girls refuse.
Then big trouble.
Lola told me how it goes.

I know staff
and I can't say
I'm glad or sad.
But Mr. M.
is there, not a
regular, but he

always seems to
show up.

Now he's cool,
doesn't rush out
the door when his
shift ends
and asks questions.
Wants to know
our story and
has a lecture for
everything,
like he could
solve my troubles.
Don't think so,
they go on and on
like a story that doesn't
end.

....

My girl's pregnant
and I can't see her,
can't talk to her,
can't write to her,
so I pray for her
and when they
come for bible class
I'll ask the sister
to say a prayer for us.

Something's gotta change.
I know it,
knew it the last time
and want this to *be*
the last time.
I can get out of this mess.

Eric did and so did Juan.
I even told my teacher
about wanting out of
the crazy
life, very crazy
because I could be dead
or in jail.

....

And what about my mother
crying at my grave or sitting
in some prison waiting area
to see me through a glass or
watching me in hand cuffs
instead of me holding her
grandchild.

Somedays I don't want out.
I want to run the streets,
be somebody,
stand on my turf and let
the world know it's mine.
I've done that since I was
11, tough very tough
and loyalty rushes through
my veins like the rapids.

Lola wants me out,
my mother wants me out.
My father was a gangbanger
before he was born, just
like his father.
Dead before I got here,
both of them.
Do I want to repeat this scene
or am I going to show up for my kid,

my son, my daughter,
lay down my guns,
bury my tattoos in piles
of diapers and learn
to read.

The gang is my family
my home.
Only 15 and already
lost 4 guys,
their blood splattered
on my heart and
chasing me in dreams
that end in stifled screams
and regret.

....

Is tomorrow a new day?
Can I crawl up through
dying spaces of hope
and move on?
Goodbye to places
and things and
my homeboys that
are etched into
the air I breathe
and the beat of my
heart.

How will I walk down the street
and who will watch my back
while I go from place to place
in search of I don't even know what.

I am ready for tomorrow
just have to pause at the
starting line,
see who shows up to help,
like I could even ask
for help.
Don't know how to.

I'm on a trip to nowhere
just this side of a sudden grave
or a career in prison,
maybe even *life* if I
don't watch things.

Lola and I gotta get out of here.
Her unit uses a lot of restraint.
Ya know.
When staff grabs you and throws you down.
Face down.
Smashing your face into the ground.
Kids call it *rug burns*.

Lola said some girl had
a face with flesh hanging out.
Took the skin right off.
Hope she closed her eyes
to that sight.
Bones get broken.
Some girl was twisted like a pretzel.
Then handcuffed and shackled.
Told her ma and she told mine.

Gotta watch your step with staff.
Some are pretty rough with kids.
Lookin' for a fight.
Big guys slammin' little kids.

Chokin' 'em, kickin' and
like they have it in for kids,
some of 'em do, not all.
A long list of hurts on the grievance form.
Gonna pray it doesn't happen to us.

Bible study could help.
Deciding to read
is calling me.
Some old guy
on Oprah learned
to read when he was
100 plus so there
 must be hope for me.

Some dopey old guy
in my neighborhood
says he hangs his hat
on hope and it works
every time.

I'm running low on
things working in my life
so for now am shaking
hands with hope,
watching for something
good to come my way.
Being a reader for starters.
Gettin' a high school diploma.
Takin' a baby class.
Being a real man.
Takin' my kid to the park.
Holding his hand when life is hard.
Wrapping my arms and heart around his.

I have a bigger part in
what's ahead than I care
to admit.
Dr. Seuss said,
*kid, you can move
mountains,* so I guess
he could mean me.

CARLOS

Carlos could live his life in confinement. He may never realize his potential. He has taken a life and lost his own. One day he will awaken to what has happened and will grieve for two lost lives. His spirit is strong and this strength will allow him to find meaning and even peace. He is deeply regretful of his crime, and prays for the victim's family with devotion. Carlos is a casualty of street life.

> *Each of us is more than the worst thing we've ever done.*
>
> — Bryan Stevenson

I am invisible.
But I made my mark.
You won't forget me.
Brown and young.
Speakin' two languages.
Smarter than you think.

Was goin' places.
You saw the spark.
I know you did.

I'll be outta here someday
I can dream.
I'm gonna pray.

I know a guy who
made it out.
Got caught up in a sad crime
as a kid.
Got grace,
now he gives it.

Big time.
Says he gives *eternal apology.*
Teacher told us about him.

Went to prison young.
Crime at 13.
Gang-related.
This is really big.
He got a college degree in prison.
Said no matter what a kid did they
deserve another chance.

Someday when I get out,
if I get out,
am gonna look him up.
Shake his hand.
Hug him.
Bless him.
Thank him.

I have a picture
in my head.
And I can see me.
Grown up.
Respectable.
A job and all that.
Family of my own.
Maybe helping someone
turn their life around.

I have something
they can't take away.
Even in this cell.
Don't know the word.
Just think it's my soul.

I'm still afraid of the dark.
But I'm getting braver.
When night comes I shudder
and then pray some.
Helps to pull the blanket over my face
and curl up into a ball.
Talkin' to myself till I drift on
to that place of nothing and quiet
I call sleep.

....

I know this homie goin' nowhere,
for *life*.
He ain't getting' out.
Well, maybe when he's 60 or 70.
Or not.
Was an honor student and artist.
Things went down in the park,
went with his homie and the dude left in a body bag.
Smoked him.
Parents adored him, now they cryin'.

One more piece cracked off teacher's heart.
Another kid, life lost.
Teacher says, *two*.
Two lives lost.
No one's coming home.
Sad story, very sad story.

Some kid's been here a long time.
I mean since 11 or 12.
Growin' up in this hell hole
with staff yellin' and carryin' on.
Yellin' for us to get out of our windows
and with mean in their words and their tones
like we're not really kids.

Just wanna see what's out there.
No harm.
Gotta watch and see.
Even an animal can see out of its cage.

Ugly words 24/7.
Chips at my steel
and strengthens it.
Can't explain it,
makes me sad and mad.
I wanted more.
Teacher says I deserve more.

One guy been here since 12
and had more codes than any one.
When the code is called everyone runs,
I mean staff, that is.
Screaming for us to get down.

Codes can be mean.
OC spray right in the eyes.
The whole canister.
Takes a long minute to recover.
Maybe some lasting damage.
I call it *blind injustice*.
Kids screaming a big agony.
No mercy.

There should be a law or something
about rinsing off the spray.
Like a shower or something.
Some kid said he got sprayed
multiple times in one day,
and staff put a towel under his door
so he'd have to breathe it over and over.
Coulda died.

I was up in Montana and heard about a kid.
He didn't want to take a shower after OC,
not with a big crowd of officers watching him,
naked and shackled.
He just washed off his face in the toilet.
Nasty.

I watch the teacher when the code call goes out.
She waits and waits for the all clear,
and then if she hears the words, "No OC used,"
she breathes a big sigh of relief.
I been watching her.
She's heard a lot of spray screamers, pretty sure.
Kids crying and yelling and squealing in pain.
Hard to watch.
Hard to hear.

Once I saw this staff
throw a kid across the room in the code.
I think that was too much.
Too much, since the kid was really small
and the staff was really big.
Really big.

Didn't see the staff back much after that.
Heard he worked somewhere else around here, not with kids.
I didn't see it but heard that some staff
pushed a kid's head into a bucket.
After the kid threw up.
I call it mean.
Maybe even cruel.
Choking and sputterin'
on his own puke.
I heard a kid say
he'd like to see staff out on the street.

No spray, just fists and revenge.
Being up in here can be bad.

....

Lots goes on around here.
One time we got locked in our class.
That coulda turned out bad.
Teacher knew it was just her and us.
Nowhere to go.

Heard her say she believes in kindness all the way.
Respect, too.
We knew it all along.
She said let's show staff who you are.
Be your best man.
Imagine your grandpa or pastor
is sitting next to you.
Or your mama.
Make 'em proud.

That's why we just kept goin' with the day.
Her respect kept us straight.
Believe me, she was safe
in those long minutes of
teacher lockdown.

Some kid up in here
had our teacher on the outs.
Was really mean to her.
Awful.
Disrespect and cruel.
Called her names.
Told her she was an old Jew lady.
Said he wished she'd die.
Threw her lunch in the trash,
dumped her stuff in the toilet.

Spit on her desk.
Big, big bully.
Got suspended.

She kept showing up.
Sayin' today's a new day.
Let's turn it around.
Get going on life.
Find a dream.
Get educated.
Find a path.
Get a mentor.
Show the world who you are.
Succeed.
Give something back.

Guess what?
I mean, almost never,
really, never,
do kids in here say *sorry*.
He did.
Said every last word and act
was a big regret.
Said he learned a lot.
Way more than book learnin'.
Looked her right in the eye
with those words.
Said sorry for her pain.
Told her she was a great teacher.
Said *thank you* for not giving up on him.
Told me they shook hands,
locked eyes.
Said she was proud.
Said she forgave him.
He told me.
Stood straight up, grinned and told me.

....

Sometimes I dream.
Take some good trips.
And even seen some homies.
Feelin safe and together.
Kickin up some fun,
even if we break the law
we're cool.

Speakin of dreams
I have some big ones.
Travelin far away from this life.
That's been pullin me down.

I see the world out there.
Makes me think I am more
than one crime.
Which I rather not say.
Or even remember.
I know was wrong.
Saying no is harder than you think.
And I have been prayin' for a better me.

See my mama cares about me.
Workin hard to take care of things.
Helpin' me with whatever.
I let her down.
Way down.
Smashing some of her dreams.
Like glass shattering.
Pieces of broken hope lying around.

I hear her cries in the night,
even from here,
and I get real quiet inside,
thinkin' about her.

That quiet feeling is deep,
and it takes me on a trip
I guess to my conscience.

Glad, so glad I see her at visits.
One of the homies has nobody.
His family cut him loose.
Just like that.
Going to prison for a minute.
And that's that.
No visits, no calls.
No love.
Disappeared.
Just disappeared.
Mean.
Just mean.

....

I hear a voice.
I think it's me
or someone wise.
Tellin' me this and that.
Places to go.
Things to learn,
who to trust,
what to do next.

Afraid of what's gonna
happen to me.
Will I get *life*,
be inside the whole time
till I'm old, really old.

My teacher says
keep reading.
Just keep reading.

Work in the prison library.
Teach everyone to read.
Maybe I will.
I lose myself in books.
And I find myself too.

I could write my own story.
A bunch of harsh words
with no ending.
Cuz I don't know how
it gonna end.

I got published in the *Beat,*
first issue at our site.
My teacher brought it over
and said, "Take a look."
I read it and cried.
Don't know why, just cried.

My father kept tellin' me
that this would happen,
I would live life in prison.
Shoulda listened, wish I did.

Teacher says I can live
life anywhere I am.
Do a dream inside,
on the outs, both.
I made a big mess of things.
Didn't listen.
Gonna pay big.

Got lots of time to think.
Sometimes I like it.
Sometimes I don't.
Saw this film at school,

The Farm.
Lots of bad news on that one.
Like if you have life,
the homies cut you loose.
Not goin' be there.
They move on.
Then, your girl cuts you loose
and all that's left is your mama.
For sure she's goin' die one day.
Then, no one, no one.

Best thing to do is pray,
then take a big breath.
And listen to that
message from my heart.

Gives me hope.
Hope is like food.
Hope is like love.
Hope is like air.
Hope keeps me goin'.
Here's what hope can do.
Let's me feel like I'm more
than that gangbangin' kid
that took someone out.
Way more.

LOLA

A troubled teen who knows how to tell her innermost thoughts and feelings, yet is frozen by the circumstances that have starved her spirit. A strength shines through, that thread of hope easily nurtured by helping hands and hearts. Lola's list of obstacles is long. Will she be another teen suicide or will she claim a place in the world as a teen mother, uneducated and feeling the sting of an incarcerated parent? Mentors must show up for Lola, or she will sink down the path of poverty and illiteracy.

> *The more that you read, the more things you will know.*
> *The more that you learn, the more places you'll go.*
> — Theodor Seuss Giesel aka *Dr.Seuss*

Here I go and is anyone listening, really listening?
I don't think so, but I want to believe.
I could be heard even if my words lie silent
on faded hopes and dark dreams, and I wait for
compassion that may or may not come.

I'm lost. I'm 16. I'm strong. I'm brave. I'm afraid.
I'm struggling to find even one piece
of me in this tangled web of misery
that inches along the road to nowhere.

....

I'm pregnant.
I'm a child to be mother and who
will hold me in the darker moments
when I'm full with you who is
just a faint seed of humanity.

In these walls of lockdown and lockup, I dream of you,
talk to you, pray for you, love you, loathe you,
beckon you, wait for you, cry for you, sing to you,

115

all the while whispering my fears to a moon I can't
see and stars that don't shine.

While jail wraps around me
you grow determined to
come here, braving this storm of chaos
that smothers and chokes me.

Your father is nowhere,
tonight in jail or in some crusty
place with guns and drugs and
too much sadness for one 15
year old boy, maybe
man who thinks you are a
sacred toy and who will both
pray and play with you.

We are lost, he and I,
you and I, in this maze
of crime and we can't even read.

My parents are together but apart.
My grandma raised me, my aunt is on drugs,
my brother is in jail, my grandpa's in his grave.

I'm afraid of the dark.
I know how to cook, but we don't have enough food.
Poverty sweeps around me
like a tornado that goes on and on.

I am pretty but I feel ugly.
My body is strong,
my mind is confused.
I have tattoos. I rescue animals,
my brother hurts them.

Someone once told me I could be someone when I was six.
I know that's a joke that sputters into the present
while I paint *dropout* on my tee shirt for all to see.

....

I found out I was pregnant
with a home kit, but no one to help celebrate.
Or catch my tears that drenched the whole place.
And now I sit on suicide watch in juvy, cries of sister rebels
stretching down the long and heartless hall.

I hear yelling, staff is perturbed.
Staff is hyped up, staff is everything
I don't want to be.

Except Ms. J and Ms. K. and Ms. D.
I think they do care and sometimes I hear
them tell one of us we could be someone or
something and not be caged like an animal
snarling and whimpering.

Karla is screaming, she won't go to school.
Her cries pierce the morning.
I cover my ears and balance my breakfast tray,
lumpy oatmeal teetering on my lap
listening to a symphony of teenage woe.

I know the school call is coming.
My red wrist band will put me right at the front so if I run
or bash my head into the concrete I'll be seen, though I have lived my
whole life without being seen.

....

Did my mother ever think
while I sat inside her womb
that one day I would be a

security risk and juvenile inmate,
tattoos running down my arms
and up my thigh, my hands
forming gang signs instead
of holding a high school diploma.

I hear them coming to unlock our doors.
My tray is still filled with overdone cereal
and I'll drop it half eaten into the trash can
with nineteen sister souls, lost like me,
with hair tied tight and high so the lice
won't hide in our heads and make our captors crazy.

He's here, Mr. G., been here forever, at least every time
I'm here and he cares about us.
He's serious about school, always nagging about reading
and finding a way to go up and out of here, out of poverty,
and crime and drugs.
I know he's proud of our deeds, our *school* deeds, our scores
rising, rising, rising.

When I read aloud he claps, even smiles at my courage
while I stumble through a paragraph with words too big
or strange or have a silent something.

He talks about us being literate.
Is that when I can fill out the application
for a job and read the doctor's orders?
Sign the rental papers and
tell my baby a story without remembering it.

He says we can learn to like learning
and we can learn to like ourselves.
Now that's a stretch for me because
what's to like?
My school reports of missed days and

failing grades and last in line to be
the teacher's pet.

He says look at the pluses.
What pluses? My life is a minus.
I'm a minus. My children will be crossed
by the minus sign, losers in a lost land.

....

No one here is special.
Except if you cut your wrists or sneak a
staple from the classroom or library.
Or carve hate into your hands
or face or knees or maybe even
a finger nail to gash your pain and
despair into flesh that has no feeling
and then feels every cut.

I heard about one girl that sliced a hole in
her hand and buried a pencil point.
The poison spilled while the kids sat on
lockdown and frantic adults searched
for one forsaken pencil.
Big drama.
Used a broken spoon to do it.
Took her right outta here.
Next stop the ER.

I look up and down the rows of desks
and see the faces of all of us who have
lost our way, stealing cars, and punching
our mothers or brothers or grandmothers.
And crawling out the window at night to
run the streets, a favorite past time and
where I find a patch of peace.

Strange and oh so very strange
that in the flood of violent nights
where innocence scatters like the stars,
I take a deep breath and find myself
in ugly tasks and risky adventures.

....

The teacher's radio announces a
Code Red, and we all jump to action.
Take off our shoes, cover our heads,
remain silent, listen for instructions,
wait for staff, who rush to our class,
herd us like sheep to our rooms,
so we don't riot and revolt.
Somewhere around here there's
a crisis, some kid flipped out.

....

The baby gives a kick she or he, not sure yet,
but my ultrasound is next week.
I found out staff has to give me snacks, or else.
The other girls are jealous.
Ms. A. gives me whole peanut butter sandwiches,
not those small cracker packages
that are almost always broken.

Just like my heart and now my mother's
heart and maybe my daddy's too.
I heard one girl had a newborn in her room
crying and crying and crying
until the train of somewhere picked her up
and down the tracks she rode.
Baby left screamin' for her mama.
Mama stayed behind.
Wailing and weeping.

I get tired when I think of all
I have to do to make life work.
School, a job, a baby, even a place
to live and someone to help me.
I can't do it by myself.
I got suicide on my mind.

Dying is my decision for me
but no way am I killing my baby.
I have to figure this out.
Who can help me untangle this mess?

I see staff every 10 minutes
on my special "watch" to make sure I don't hurt myself.
Like I heard really did happen and someone hanged herself
with the bed sheet.
Don't they know I would never kill myself in here.
Not until I have a chance to see Angel and my grandma.
And my baby.

Grandma.
She is everything to me all wrapped up in a tiny self
of kindness and questions.
She rescued me from parents who couldn't figure
out what I needed, or even what they needed,
and talk about lost, are they ever.
I wonder if jail is in the genes. If so, I don't have a chance.

If the judge sends me home Grandma will help me.
Is she too old to take care of me and my baby?
Will she tell me or will she wait
till I lie bleeding with wrists spurting blood
across a kitchen too empty to call home and too bare
for one more mouth.

....

Rosa is a good homie in here.
I'd even let her sing to my baby.
And we could talk about names.
Maybe we would be best friends
and I could let her hold the baby.
Like Ms. C. says, get lots of
helpers, friends, relatives, mentors.
I don't have to be like the homie who
went to jail right after birth.
Not even two days and she
was nursing the baby *after* using drugs.
I think maybe the baby was in the hospital and
she was in jail with a breast pump and a tub of tears.

....

My P.O. had me talk to a social worker
who wants me to think about adoption.
Giving my baby a good home
with some people I can meet.
She says my baby would have a good life.
I can't even imagine giving my kid to someone to keep.

Maybe I am young, but I know the best place
for a baby is with the mama.
I bet my baby loves me already.
Knows my scent.
Knows my voice.
Knows my heartbeat.
How could we say goodbye?

Cary is adopted.
My cousin's best friend.
She even knows.
I asked her if she wants to meet her first mother
and she said "No way am I gonna meet that bitch."
Cary is always angry and in trouble.

At least she could meet her mother.
I read about someone who
was left in a gas station bathroom.
Newborn, just left and she grew up not
knowing her birthday.

I told the social worker to talk to me in September
cuz I'm not ready to think about adoption.
That word gives me a scare.
I may not have much.
No education, no money but I know how to love.

There's a place I can go,
where I can learn to be a real mother.
My baby can come too,
for two years and we can grow up together.

I could teach my baby to be special,
not to grow up like me.
Rolling my eyes at adults,
spreading rumors, bullying kids,
fighting, stealing and saying a million *no's*
when *yes* sits on my tongue
like a smoldering fire.

....

I wish I could write Angel a letter,
but no way cuz he's on probation
and it's forbidden, even if he is the *baby daddy.*
When I talk to my grandma she can
tell me if he's home or in juvy.
Wherever he is, he's thinking of me.

My grandma likes Angel.
She heard him telling me about
wanting to leave his gang and

planning to be a real daddy.
I'm not sure what that is.
But it could be when a baby
needs help or comfort or food or
whatever else, he is there.
How is Angel going to get
out of the gang?
We'll have to run and hide
and what about the part
where he tells me his gang
is like a drug, pulling him,
calling him, wrapping around
him like a cloud of bliss?

I don't know anyone who got out
except for Chivo in that book
about gangs that my teacher
goes on and on and on about.
East Side Stories.
You gotta read it.
And a few authors who wrote about
escaping gang life and now they
are preaching about the whole thing.

Could my Angel be strong enough to
walk away from something that
keeps his heart beating?

My teacher showed a few movies about gangs.
I wanted to watch and I wanted to run.
Too many boys hurt and killed, even a girl.
I saw that picture of the baby in the coffin
from a drive-by and my skin jumped.
I felt like throwing up more than
like morning sickness.
Sick to the bone, to the farthest place

inside me where a block of fear sits
like lead while I shiver and shake.

....

Tonight is visits
and that means Grandma.
She never misses
and drops off her smile that
may last the whole week.
She doesn't want me to be here.
In her eyes I'm not a real criminal.
Just have some things to learn
and am running behind.

I'm glad we get to go outside before dark.
I need to see the sky.
Feel the fresh air,
watch the day glow by.
Even through prison wire
I see the beauty and peace
and hope and comfort.
The touch of the sun
on my shoulders and face
brings a sigh that drapes
me in mercy.

Epilogue

*But simply punishing the broken – walking away
from them or hiding them from sight – only ensures
that they remain broken as we do, too. There is no
wholeness outside of our reciprocal humanity.*
— Bryan Stevenson

The screams of youth in the booking cells never quiet in my mind. Haunting and shocking, they replay over and over, shouting out an appalling, crushing and dispiriting ordeal. My tears well from a pool of empathy and anguish. The images and sounds linger and give rise to a compelling, urgent passion for transformation.

A broken system brings deeper ruptures to kids that have arrived, sometimes in pieces, and are held together only by pure will and mercy. Cries in the night can become fury by day. In this setting we strive to educate and amend suffering, a daunting job amid untold hurdles.

Thousands of children have come through the doors during my tenure. Too many will march forward to adult incarceration in a national crisis of kids in jail. The legacy of broken lives begets further breaks. One by one we seek to provide moments that transcend. Two stories come to mind and unveil the triumph and tragedy of incarceration.

When Alonso said that he knew he was a *good kid*, I wanted to bow to him. I knew that comment was his transforming moment. I knew he would take it from there. As I learned more of his story, I marveled at such resilience and courage.

I was awed to see Alonso stand and face life full steam and on his own, without the support of family or loved ones. His life on the streets included learning English, finding foster care, time in juvenile detention, and then finding out that all along he was and is *a good kid*. I cried when he left; sorrow for what was behind and joy for what could be ahead. Alonso will make it. He will carve a life with meaning and goodness. He embodies the term *spirit soldier*. I hope to see him on a college campus, where I visit to talk about juvenile justice and correctional education. There he'll be, attending classes, or teaching classes. Or at a local library, with his kids, at a special program for toddlers, giving them the gift of literacy and love, all at once. I'll listen to Alonso share about his life, and the miles upon miles between himself and the long-standing hurdles. That now he walks on solid ground with dreams that have come alive in all the glory of family, career, health and happiness, the pursuit of which was obscured by those early beginnings, now laid to rest with arms to embrace his future.

But not Daniel. His story chills. Brilliant, lost, fragile and with severe mental challenges, he was both frightening and inspiring to have in the classroom. He could be furious, respectful, hopeful, and he was crushed by his hardships and traumas. As many youth, Daniel left detention with no life plan and with a wild rage. Living on the streets, searching for direction, calling the classroom for love, for support and for hope, he continued to spiral downstream. Some years after his juvy exit, I received a letter, telling me of family deaths, one from the hood and one from a hospital, and that he, Daniel, was in prison. He asked if I could send books.

I have met many Daniel's in the past year, working in a special literacy program with maximum security kids. Week after week we walk through stories that enlighten, inspire, give rise to deep and critical thinking, and to empathy, the true ticket to a positive adulthood.

Empathy builds spirit soldiers. To abandon their street soldier badges, these warriors must live from the place of community and compassion. Watching the process unfold is remarkable, extraordinary. To see compassion emerge in listening to a peer's story, a tale in a book we share, or something I present stirs all present. The kids are right, I am honored, and I am humbled to be their teacher, their guide, and their mentor as they reach for a life with purpose, a life with respect, and a life without bars. I dedicate the words in this work to each of them. May our compassion and guidance become their village of hope, promise, purpose and deliverance.

Afterword

There are times when we are powerless to prevent injustice, but there must never be a time when we fail to protest.

— Elie Wiesel

Redesigning a system fractured by a multitude of hurdles seems impossible in the culture and climate of an enduring doctrine. The Code of Silence prevails, now so normalized as to be enshrined as a part of the gatekeepers' orthodoxy. Reporting mistreatment, in most instances, results in an inside investigation. Observable changes do not occur. A host of reformers stand ready from all corners of advocacy. The court, educators, legislators, current president Barack Obama, and other juvenile justice factions rise in devoted missions to turn the tide for kids in custody. But emergency measures are needed. Kids cannot wait and many will not survive the inhumanity of incarceration.

Solitary confinement, withholding of educational services, food deprivation, mental health urgencies, staff brutalities, extreme isolation, gang retaliation, and family disruption continue day-to-day with no reprieve. Children already damaged by early life circumstances cannot navigate these horrors without incurring further and often lasting wounds.

Violations of ethics and human decency appall. Delaying or denying the use of an inhaler, disregarding cries and threats of suicide, ignoring mental health outbursts, and treating children as dissolute offenders, as unredeemable criminals, and as unworthy of respect and compassion, allow and perpetuate systemic suffering. These realities are not isolated events, but rather reflect the pandemic *injustice* of a juvenile justice system.

Although crimes have occurred, respect, compassion, and fair sentencing will urge kids to pursue decent lives, rather than bearing the current crude and heartless practices. Who will speak up for children who are violated in numerous ways from a tarnished court event to a detention experience that may, for so many, end in adult incarceration? *Children* moved to adult court, *children* sentenced to adult prison, and *children* given lifetime sentences in spite of being *children*, with all the considerations of neurology and psychology, perpetuate a cycle that brutalizes youth.

Some have asked, "Has the system changed? Have reforms emerged?" I say, "Yes!" There are schools that reverse the cycle of school failure and street culture. Yes, there are juvenile jails that provide humane practices, though the exception. Enlightened programs offset the hopelessness, the culture of poverty, and deficits so vast that only the most devoted efforts can renovate these youthful lives. Yet, shackles, staff-on-youth violence, cries of youth, and the ever-present despair hasten desolation amid the ruthless culture of retribution. The transformation we seek must be the rule and not the exception. Advances must replace the punitive and cruel models that continue to hold strong, even as reform is hailed.

We are a nation disgraced in regard to our children at risk...broken minds, hearts, and spirits line the hallways at juvenile detention centers across our land. Racial disparity prevails. Youth of color crowd court school classrooms with a disproportionate and disgraceful actuality.

One by one, innovative programs rise and alter the cycle of anguish. From chamber music in Santa Cruz, California to exemplary educational programs in D.C., the course is changing. Across the nation creative, committed, and compassionate advocates are erasing indignities and ushering in humanity. Pioneering interventions chart the landscape of facilities that historically have held tightly to the punitive model of juvenile injustice.

Even so, a fading standard of punishment, disrespect and cruelty cannot dim in time for currently incarcerated youth. The changes, though strongly embraced by dedicated agents, cannot protect these youth who now fall prey to the pervasive carnage with its brutal and smoldering ash. As we turn to a humane standard for juvenile justice, the perpetual code of silence must be laid to rest. The fervent voices of reform echo across the nation with a resonance of compassion, restorative justice and rehabilitation, standing strong in the spirit of honoring our youth. Our kids, with their untold gifts, must emerge in a system that sees and protects their hearts, minds and spirits. And their lives. May each child be acknowledged with our respect, wisdom, best practices, humanity, and above all, our resolute efforts for true and enduring juvenile justice.

Postscript

*The song of celebration harmonizes with gratitude
for clemency and mercy.*

As *Kids in Jail* traveled to press, cardinal decisions were handed down on behalf of criminal and juvenile justice. The U.S. Supreme Court's ruling to retroactively review life without parole for inmates sentenced as juveniles, *Montgomery v. Louisiana, 2016,* to Barack Obama's ban on solitary confinement for juveniles in federal prison, resounded in advocacy venues and within prison walls alike. These constitutive decisions rushed into the hearts, minds and spirits of incarcerated men and women throughout the nation, alighting hope and the prospect for mercy. Numerous inmates, incarcerated during their childhoods, have lived with the notion that their last breath would be inside prison walls, *and* others have lived with the savage, life-threatening practice of solitary confinement.

From every corner of the nation, and in solidarity with voices from around the world, these decisions are being proclaimed for their humanity and for long-awaited justice. As this opportunity for a life without bars advances, the clock is moving for lifers. Some, in their 60's and 70's, having spent a half century in prison, cannot afford long delays in the review process. Others, with fewer decades of confinement, can embrace the dream of taking their places in families, in communities, and in the pursuit of life with grace. As the reviews ensue, the ethics and agendas of the reviewers can become either a dire defeat or exoneration for those anxiously awaiting release. As we celebrate judicial transformation, we must work fiercely to educate those who will ultimately determine the destiny of each inmate in pursuit of amnesty and justice.

Gratitudes

As we express our gratitude, we must never forget that the highest appreciation is not to utter words but to live by them.

— John F. Kennedy

My first and supreme gratitude goes to the kids. They have been *my* teacher for fifteen years, *inside.* I have learned those beautiful lessons about love, compassion, passion and dedication. My heart is theirs. I am grateful to my probation partners. Some are exceptional, shaping progressive changes and programs, and serving with integrity, dedication, and compassion. Sharing partnership cultivates a bridge of service and collaboration for kids with such high need. I have found kinship with those that are deeply committed to their wards, our kids. To the *others*, I have found purpose, to be part of the community of juvenile justice reform. The screamers, the transgressors, and the degraders have been my call to action. I thank them. To Dr. Scott Wyatt, educator extraordinaire, thank you for your incomparable enlightenment. And for guiding me in delivering first-rate programs. Your brilliance lights the way. I honor your heart and your service. To my court school colleagues, I have learned so much in your presence and in our community. We hold the torch of hope for discarded kids. Appreciation and respect to Judge Marsha Slough, Judge Lynn Poncin, Terrance Stone, Dr. Jennifer Tilton, Bobbi Caldwell, Attorneys Carlos Perez, Tamara Ross, and Jonathan Simon. All dedicated leaders and exemplars in their respective fields. Each one bringing us closer to attaining justice in this world. Deep appreciation to Professors Tamar Birckhead, J.D. and to Mae Quinn, J.D., fierce advocates for juvenile justice and profound educational leaders. Their gifts humble us. Their eminence, praiseworthy practice, and devotion will impact generations of children in custody. Thank you to Richard Ross for his *Juvenile In Justice* project that fuels my passion to continue the daunting work of juvenile justice reform. And for the gift of a poignant photo. To Dr. Lesley Farmer, an exceptional educational leader, librarianship educator, mentor, friend, comrade in literacy for marginalized youth. Appreciation to my long-time colleagues, Drs. Carolyn Eggelston, Thom Gehring, and Randall Wright, all opening my eyes and mind to the heartbeat of correctional education. My unlimited regard and appreciation to Bart Lubow for a lifetime of supreme devotion to juvenile justice. He has awakened advocacy from coast to coast. My gratefulness to Bethany and Robin Casarjian for creating *Power Source* and Lionheart Foundation. Their work is devotion and love and wisdom and grace. Appreciation and deep respect to Bob Riha Jr. for his contribution of a photo that speaks to posterity. To my beloved first mentor, Dr. Sidney Simon, who taught me way back in the day how to do things in education. My first students, now in their late 50's and 60's still remember the power of Sid's process and the enduring transformation of our work together. My true thanks to Daniel Ortega, mentor and colleague for his grace and heart. Thanks to Ken Decroo, mentor, fellow author and partner in service to at-risk learners. And to Mike Lepore, a distant educator in miles, though in spirit and practice sharing a profound solidarity. Gratitude to Anthony DiMartino, Porscha Guillot, and Kaitlin Wright, the new generation of justice advocates, inspiring with their extraordinary gifts. To my dear friends who are family — Julieanne Collins, Barbara Frances, Carol Pedder, and Megan Smith. Thank you for putting your stamps of love and wisdom on this book. Gratitude to Doreen Ramsey for being a steadfast hand in stormy times as I wove my way through the tangles of health woes and publishing delays. To Elisa Gusdal for directing me to stand tall for truth; both modeling devotion to education and commitment to equity and educators. I am privileged to be their colleague. Acknowledgment to Renee Lewis for bringing wisdom and calm to the stormy waters of birthing this book. Special thanks to Almyra Moore, my dedicated colleague, a kindred warrior for transformation. Great thanks to Amy Cheney, master librarian, a true spirit of devotion to literacy and kids in need. Grace to Mary Beth Tinker for her courage and conviction that brought her all the way to the U.S. Supreme Court for First Amendment Rights as a young student, reminding me of this timeless right. Deep appreciation to my partners in justice service.

Some new to me, and all strongly established in justice reform, all humbling in such profound efforts for humanity: Nate Balis, Cindy Sanford, Eugene Brown, Xavier McElrath-Bey, and Steve Nawojczyk. To authors Carissa Phelps, Jimmy Santiago Baca, Luis J. Rodriguez, Jesse De LaCruz, and to journalist Carmilla Floyd and photojournalist Joseph Rodriguez; thank you all for being my curriculum and inspiration. To the late Sherman Bell, Michael Long and Lula Thornton, officers of the highest eminence, and gifted mentors. Your inspiration was momentous. Warm thanks to journalist Rosemary Jenkins for getting the editing process in motion. A world of thanks to Linda Prentice, fellow educator and editor, blending grace, respect and her gift of language and love. Profound gratitude to Dawn Fischle for her creative contributions to KIJ, given with grace. Special appreciation to Cynthia Cummings for her artistic guidance for the cover. To Dee Gerken, keeper of the updated files, well of compassion for the grim discoveries of injustice, and sister warrior to right the wrongs. To my cherished sisters, Barbara Guttman MacDougall and Patricia Guttman Meyer, awesome editors and devoted to seeing the project to the last page with love. Gratitude for months of all-day dates with words. I am awed by their deep understanding of what this book means to me. To my remarkable kids, Mark Rapparport, Julie Stenger, Josh Stenger, all rich gifts for changing the world. All dazzlers in this world, stepping up with their brilliance, and cheerleading. Gratitude to my daughter via marriage, Shannon Dolan for her thought-provoking questions and her love. To my partner, Leslie Fisher Becker, for being a gracious doula in birthing this book. And for asking such important questions in the search for truth and justice. A well of gratitude to the imprisoned beings on this earth. As you stand in the darkness of incarceration you are not forgotten.

In Memoriam

Remembering these children and youth who have lost their lives in custody or related to custody.

> *The bitterest tears shed over graves are for words*
> *left unsaid and deeds left undone.*
> — Harriet Beecher Stowe

Alex
Andre
Andy
Brandon
Daniel
Dion
Eric
Isiah
Jake
Jonathan
Kalief
Kindra
Martin
Nicholaus
Rosemary
Victoria

… and so many others, unnamed here, who have perished during confinement. Giving tribute to each one and with hope that their lost lives may usher in profound reform. May each one be remembered with our respect and compassion, and with our commitment to preclude future suffering and loss of life.

About the Author

I must uphold my ideals, for perhaps the time will come when I shall be able to carry them out.
— Anne Frank

Jane Guttman's steadfast symphony with kids began in 1967 as a student teacher stumbling in a setting with infinitely high stakes for youth. Her fervent journey with reluctant learners, and her persistent passion for educating troubled children have followed her as she continues to champion marginalized kids with a fierce and bold spirit, working for system transformation and justice.

Jane has taught humanistic education and communication skills training to parents, counselors, educators, and students, and has been an adjunct professor at California State University. She has been a keynote speaker in various venues, and a workshop facilitator for the American Adoption Congress and California School Library Association. As an instructional leader, she actively advocates for pioneering practices to provide all incarcerated learners with access to literacy. Jane advocates for imprisoned learners and promotes social emotional learning in a setting that endorses and delivers retribution. Her influence and rapport with kids in custody, her comprehensive experience with esteem development, and her devotion to multiculturalism contribute to Jane's effective teaching practice and her gift for redirecting, motivating, and inspiring our troubled urban youth. Her innate belief in the virtue and potential of all human beings inspires staff and youth. Jane's work with jailed children has blazed a trail for best practices in the realm of educational and social justice.

Jane contributed to a textbook for a correctional education advanced degree program, "Teaching in the Existential Village," *In the Borderlands*, 2006. She has authored "Books Behind Bars," *Last Bell* in a 2006 issue for *NEA Today*, and "Reading to Freedom," *California School Library Journal*, 2008. She has penned poems for *Digital Inclusion*, 2008, a book that promotes literacy services for marginalized youth, and has authored *The Gift Wrapped in Sorrow*, 1999; as a poet-writer-author, she has been in love with words for over a half century. Jane lives in a rural California community.

Kickstarter Gratitude

Thank you for your very kind monetary support to *Kids in Jail*. I am ever grateful.

Elizabete Almeida
Sue Apostoli
Alan Bennett
Jerilyn Bodemar
Lesley Bogad
Cookie Braude
Katie Grace Bell
Ali Bueno
Carol Chandler
Julieanne Collins
Madeleine DeGarmo
Alain Descouches
Jan Destazio
Anthony DiMartino
Shannon Dolan
Carmilla Floyd
Joanna Folino
Dee Gerken
Jan Winslow-Dillon
Bette and Mel Goldsmith
Perry Haberman
Addy Jimenez Haga
Marina Handwerk
Rosemary Jenkins
Cristen Kilpatrick
Patty Martin
Edward Martinez
Barbara MacDougall
Erin MacDougall
Carolyn McWilliams
Patricia Meyer
Diana Nice-Michel
Elisa Miller

Al Moore
Beth Mulligan
Barbara Murray
Bob Pearl
Jeremy Pearl
Carol J. Pedder
Lynn O. Peterson
Kathleen Prentice
Linda and Robert Prentice
Dan Prozinski
Mark Rapparport
Duncan Rayside
Jendi Reiter
Brad Roberts
Isabelle Rosenlund
Sheri Ross
Sally Riggs
Rhonda and Bruce Smith
Josh Stenger
Julie Stenger
Liz Porter
Anne Provax
Lela Scott
Mark Shandrow
Aaron Sheanin
Peter Sipkins
Sharron Swan
Megan Smith
Kaitlin Wright
Scott Wyatt
Susan Yenchick
Carol Zulman